FROM ONE

BROTHER

TO ANOTHER

VOLUME 2

FROM ONE

BROTHER

TO ANOTHER

VOICES OF AFRICAN
AMERICAN MEN

EDITED BY
JEREMIAH A. WRIGHT JR.

JUDSON PRESS
VALLEY FORGE

FROM ONE BROTHER TO ANOTHER, VOLUME 2
VOICES OF AFRICAN AMERICAN MEN

Library of Congress Cataloging-in-Publication Data
(Revised for volume 2)

From one brother to another : voices of African American men / vol. 2 edited by Jeremiah A. Wright Jr. / vol. 1 edited by William J. Key and Robert Johnson-Smith II
     p. cm.
ISBN 0-8170-1250-8 (paperback : alk. paper, vol. 1)
ISBN 0-8170-1362-8 (paperback : alk. paper, vol. 2)
1. Afro-American men—Conduct of life. 2. Afro-American men—Religious life. 3. Meditations. I. Wright, Jeremiah A., Jr.
E185.86.F78 2003
242'.6—dc20
                                    96-17932

Printed in Canada
08 07 06 05 04 03 02
10 9 8 7 6 5 4 3 2 1

CONTENTS

≋

INTRODUCTION

African American men in the Christian church are often called the "silent minority." Many persons, from scholars in the academy to Monday-morning quarterbacks in the barbershops, consider the black church to be the domain of African American women. Most black churches can only boast of a male membership that ranges from 25 percent to 33 percent of the congregation.

Unfortunately, those lopsided numbers have left a negative taste in the mouths of too many men. That negative taste is made manifest either in misogynous ministries or churches where women are told to "keep silent." Or, the men who are in churches where women are affirmed feel as if they are put down and too often fall silent when they should be speaking words of encouragement, both to their sisters and to their brothers who walk and work beside them in the body of Christ.

Prayer life, a devotional life, the cultivation of a personal relationship with Jesus Christ, and the development of the soul's inward journey are often exercises that are engaged in, therefore, in a solitary fashion. There is no male-to-male bonding or encouragement. What the men do they do in silence! That is how they have earned the name "the silent minority."

From One Brother to Another is an attempt to take a step in addressing that void and breaking that silence. The following devotional meditations and reflections are written by African American men who make up that "silent minority." These are men of faith who are clergy and laity. They are officers in churches and they are "pew members" in churches. They cover a wide range of professions and occupations and they cover just as wide a range in terms of their ages and their backgrounds.

They all share in common, however, a personal relationship with the Lord Jesus Christ, a commitment to the church of Jesus Christ, and a devotion to the One who loves us unconditionally. The meditations these men write are written "from one brother to another!"

It is our hope that these meditations will help the millions of African American men in the church to find their voices and to hear a word of encouragement from those who share a common experience with them as African American men living in North America in the opening days of the twenty-first century.

It is also our hope that the women who read these pages will catch a glimpse of the "interiority" of the men they walk beside and sleep beside, yet whose true inside they do not know! To use Howard Thurman's terminology, it is our prayer that both the men and women whose hearts will be inspired by these spiritual reflections will catch a glimpse of the "nerve center of consent" that has been touched by the heart of God and blessed by the grace of God.

May your journey inward and your journey onward be enriched by what these brothers share in the following pages.

Pastor Jeremiah A. Wright Jr.
Trinity United Church of Christ
Chicago, Illinois

Marvin A. McMickle

≋

IT'S NEVER TOO LATE TO FOLLOW YOUR DREAMS

Abram was seventy-five years old when he departed from Haran. (Genesis 12:4)

How old is too old to begin a new and challenging undertaking? When is it too late to get started on a grand adventure? In the story of Abram, the most notable thing is not simply that he started out from Haran toward an unknown destination, but that he was already an old man when he left Haran to start a new chapter in his life. Abram could rightly have urged God to choose some younger and more energetic prospect for the task that God had in mind. Who would have blamed Abram if he had protested, telling God that it was too late in life for him to start something new?

Maybe there is something you always wanted to do and always meant to do, but other things kept getting in the way. Was it starting your own business, changing careers, continuing your education, or running for public office? Perhaps now the opportunity to do it has come along, but you think it is too late to consider anything so daring. If Abram could respond to the call of God at seventy-five, is it really too late for you?

I began my Ph.D. education when I was forty-two years old and finished when I was forty-eight. Most of the students who marched alongside me in the commencement processional were younger than me by a generation. So, too, were some of the instructors and professors. I had attempted to earn my Ph.D. earlier in life but was unable to finish. When I came to Cleveland, Ohio, another opportunity presented itself. I wondered if it was too late for me to start such a project, but I realized that if Abram could trust God and begin something new at seventy-five, surely it was not too late for me.

Is there a dream you have always wanted to pursue, but now you wonder if it is too late? Are you afraid you are too old to start something new? Take heart and take action. Abram did not leave Haran until he was seventy-five years old. Forget about your age and follow your dreams.

, , ,

PRAYER: *Lord, help me be open to opportunities for me to pursue my dreams or to respond to your unexpected claim upon my life. Should you do so, give me the faith and courage to believe that it is not too late to begin a new chapter in my life. Amen.*

Gordon S. Houston

FREE AT LAST

But you are a chosen race, a royal priesthood, a holy nation, God's own people, in order that you may proclaim the mighty acts of him who called you out of darkness into his marvelous light. Once you were not a people, but now you are God's people; once you had not received mercy, but now you have received mercy. (1 Peter 2:9–10)

It was while I was a student at Harvard Divinity School in the early seventies that I really came to grips with "the race issue." Or perhaps I should say I truly began to face it head on. You see, I hated the so-called "white people," sociologically known as Caucasians, because of what they had done to my people. They had lynched them. They had castrated them. They had lied about it.

But at Harvard Divinity School, early one morning, I had just finished reading a book by Paul Tillich called *The Courage to Be*. I went for a walk across the Harvard yard, and while I was walking, a heavy load too great to bear came crashing down on me. Hate was causing death in my soul. Then a voice spoke to me, which I believed to be the Holy Spirit. The voice reminded me that I am God's child and cannot live with hate. It was then and there that I gave up the hate in my soul, and I have been free ever since.

Now I know, and you ought to know too, brother, that we are of a chosen generation. You and I are members of a royal priesthood, citizens of a holy nation. We are God's own special people who have been called out of darkness into marvelous light. Therefore we love, and are loved. We forgive, and are forgiven. There is strength in knowing who we are: strong, courageous brothers, living in the midst of racism, yet overcoming it on a daily basis because of who we are in Christ—Christ, who is also our elder brother.

, , ,

ON THIS DAY: *I resolve to be free from the crippling demon of racism and to continually remember that I am a member of a royal priesthood, a holy nation, a chosen generation, God's own special people.*

E. Anthony Preston

≋

COUNTING THE COST

So I said, "The thing that you are doing is not good. Should you not walk in the fear of our God, to prevent the taunts of the nations our enemies? Moreover I and my brothers and my servants are lending them money and grain. Let us stop this taking of interest. Restore to them, this very day, their fields, their vineyards, their olive orchards, and their houses, and the interest on money, grain, wine, and oil that you have been exacting from them." (Nehemiah 5:1-19)

Uncle Tom. Most black brothers and sisters who were self-proclaimed "revolution planners" in the sixties would have done anything to avoid being called this unflattering name. Our perceptions of the name quickly change, however, when we know the factual story of the legendary slave, Uncle Tom.

Rev. Josiah Henson, the historical Uncle Tom, was a strong, courageous man. Like Nehemiah, he gained the confidence of his master and soon became invaluable. But also like Nehemiah, Henson was not comfortable being better off than most others in servitude. Unlike the fictitious Uncle Tom, whose misguided loyalty was rewarded by death at his cruel master's hands, Henson escaped to Canada with his family via the Underground Railroad. In Canada, Henson became an abolitionist, a preacher, and a successful businessman. He, along with other slaves and abolitionists, bought 200 acres of land, and like Nehemiah, was instrumental in building a new community and a new way of life. In 1849, upon meeting fellow abolitionist Harriet Beecher Stowe, Henson told her his story, which Stowe turned into the fictitious story of Uncle Tom that caused the name to carry such a negative connotation.

Both Henson and Nehemiah refused to adopt the tactics of their masters by exploiting others, and both were vehement about keeping their word. As leaders in our respective venues, you and I have the responsibility to make sure that nobody is disadvantaged by our words and deeds. We will not all become legendary, but we can still be builders in the lives of many.

, , ,

PRAYER: *Father, create in me a servant's heart and help me to refuse to exploit those who suffer. Amen.*

Kirk Byron Jones

≋

LEAN INTO YOUR POWER

Then God said, "Let us make humankind in our image, according to our likeness; and let them have dominion...." (Genesis 1:26)

My wife and I enjoy a brisk three-mile walk at the beginning of each day—a mile to the track, a mile at the track, and a mile going back home. While at the track, we often jog the curves, and that is when my two-word declaration usually kicks in: I choose. First step, "I"; second step, "choose." Next step, "I"; following step, "choose." Around the curves I go to the mental beat of "I choose," "I choose," "I choose."

How often do you feel overwhelmed by the demands you place on yourself and those placed on you by family, friends, coworkers, and life in general? The real problem is not everything that's being asked of you; it's forgetting that you have the power to choose how you will respond to everything that's being asked of you. Claiming your ability to choose is the dynamic difference between feeling pushed and pulled all the time and intentionally living—sometimes dancing, even—to the rhythm of holy empowerment.

This brings us to a fundamental question: *Who is in charge in your life?* Many persons surrender most of their power to authority figures and institutions. Though they may complain about the excessive demands placed on them by those authorities, the fact is they prefer that stress to the laborious, albeit liberating, work of self-determination.

Other persons feel impotent when it comes to taking charge of their lives. They feel weakness in the face of opportunities to exert mental and verbal force. Perhaps the malady was named by Nelson Mandela as he exhorted a people not to break under the weight of internalized oppression, saying, "Our deepest fear is not that we are inadequate. Our deepest fear is that we are powerful beyond measure. It is our light, not our darkness, that most frightens us."

Another reason many resist the power of choice is that they do not believe it is theirs to wield. For example, some Christians have a way of practicing the faith that vests God alone with power. Persons testify about "turning problems over to God" and "waiting for God to move" in this or that matter. I do not mean to condemn this sentiment, especially when what is behind it is an abiding loyalty to God's sovereignty. But one need not abandon personal power out of respect for God. In Genesis 1:26, power or "dominion" is a gift that God gives humanity. Leaning into our power, our personal choice-making capacity, is one of the countless ways we show God gratitude.

The next time you turn something over to God or ask God to decide something for you, wait a moment. You may hear God say gently but firmly, "Deal with it. I am with you, and I will help you, but dare to decide and live responsibly with the results of your choice. If I wanted to do it all by myself, I would not have created you in the first place, especially with all the abilities and gifts I have placed inside of you. Besides, I love to see you engaging challenges, creating possibilities, and choosing between options. I love watching you grow."

, , ,

ON THIS DAY: *I will embrace my personhood, claim my confidence, and lean into my power.*

Darryl D. Sims

≈≈≈

LOVE

And this is my prayer, that your love may overflow more and more with knowledge and full insight to help you to determine what is best, so that in the day of Christ you may be pure and blameless, having produced the harvest of righteousness that comes through Jesus Christ for the glory and praise of God. (Philippians 1:9-11)

So often we view love as an emotion that we either feel or don't feel, or a word that we either say or don't say. Yet love is neither an emotion nor a word. Love is God in action for a purpose. As such, love has both form and function that go beyond mere emotionalism and empty words. In 1 John 4:8, we learn that God is love. In 1 Corinthians 13:4-8, Paul outlines the characteristics of love, which are the same as the characteristics of God.

In Philippians 1:9-11, Paul gives a brief synopsis of the function of love. He writes to the church at Philippi with his prayer that their love would "overflow...with knowledge and full insight to help [them]...determine what is best...." Love leads us to seek out all there is to know about another person and gives us the insight we need to understand what we have learned. Love comes first, and with love comes knowledge and understanding.

As is typical with humanity, we've got it backwards. The world tells us that we have to know someone in order to love them. We apply this backwards thinking to our relationship with God as well as to our relationships with other people. However, we also know that the wisdom of this world is foolishness with God (1 Corinthians 3:19). Using Paul's words as our guide, we understand that our love for God is what draws us deeper into the knowledge of him. That knowledge will help us discern what is holy and will keep us primed for use by God.

This same dynamic works in our human relationships. If we begin with the love that comes from God (1 John 4:7), that love will compel us to know and understand our loved ones. It is through the eyes of God's love that we see into each other's needs and can minister reconciliation, grace, and mercy to one another. By putting love—God in action for a purpose—at the beginning of our interactions with others, we open ourselves up to be holy agents of his will, instruments for his glory, and conduits of his Spirit for the transformation of the world in preparation for his promised return.

, , ,

PRAYER: *Holy Spirit of God, help me this day to look through the eyes of your love, and to allow love to feed my desire for knowledge and understanding of you and others. May others know that I am your son by the love I show in ministering to those around me. In Jesus' name, Amen.*

James E. Sturdivant

≋

I'll Fix It!

Cast all your anxiety on him, because he cares for you.
(1 Peter 5:7)

Many brothers don't like to go to the doctor. We argue that there's nothing wrong with us, that the doctor doesn't know what to do, and that if there is a problem, we're men and we can fix it ourselves. All we have to do is take a look at how African American men are being taken out by prostate cancer, high blood pressure, and heart disease. Those statistics alone tell us that there are some things we just can't fix on our own. The time is going to come—if it hasn't already—when we don't have the answers to all our problems. We will take one look at our lives and see that there are some issues we just can't handle.

So what do we do with the problems we can't fix, the problems that make us get drunk, get high, or not come home on a given day? The Bible reminds us that we can trust God to handle every area of our lives. When we run out of answers, he is the beginning of wisdom. No matter what we're up against, God is able to fix the things that face us every day. All God asks us to do is let go of our grip and place everything in his hands.

, , ,

PRAYER: *Lord, thank you that you can handle everything that comes into my life. Help me to look to you for my answers. Help me to release and let you fix my problems for me. Amen.*

Guy S. Schley

≋

A WALK WITH GOD

Enoch walked with God; then he was no more, because God took him. (Genesis 5:24)

In a myriad of ways, God has extended the invitation to walk with him as we navigate this labyrinth called life, and it is only when we walk with God that we are able to handle the vicissitudes of life with hope and possibility. We are blessed to have Enoch as a shining example of a man who walked with God.

We have very few details about the life of Enoch, besides that he lived to be 365 years of age. One would think there would be volumes of commentaries on the life of a person who lived so long. Martin Luther King Jr. reminds us, however, that "the measure of a person's life is not in how long they live, but how well they live." We do know one thing concerning Enoch's life: he walked with God. Within this one simple but profound fact, we find endless possibilities and inferences.

First, it is inferred that Enoch had an intimate relationship with God. Many of us are only acquainted with God. Enoch steps out of antiquity to inform, inspire, and empower us to have a deeper relationship with God. We must love God as savior, and we must submit and surrender to the lordship of God just as Enoch did. It is vital that we have an intimate relationship with God to aid us through the maladies and calamities of this life.

Second, it is inferred that as Enoch and God walked, they talked. Sociologists and clinical therapists inform us that it is impossible to have a healthy, meaningful, love relationship without dialogue. Because we know Enoch was intimate with God, we know he not only walked, but also talked with God. We must do so as well if we desire a deeper relationship with God.

Third, it is inferred that Enoch was obedient to God. Enoch appears in Genesis 5:24, and he is also spoken of again in Hebrews 11:5: "By faith Enoch was taken so that he did not experience death; and 'he was not found, because God had taken him.' For it was attested before he was taken away that 'he had pleased God.'"

At best, our obedience is usually utilitarian. When we want something from God, we become as obedient as the Pharisees. The Psalmist says, "Take delight in the LORD, and he will give you the desires of your heart" (Psalm 37:4). God has the means to grant us the desires of our heart if our ways please him—not just because we want something, but because we delight in obeying his Word.

Enoch was commended as one who pleased God. At the end of his life, he was taken and was no more. We, too, will someday be no more. How will our epitaphs read?

, , ,

PRAYER: *Our God and our Father, we thank you for Enoch's life and legacy, which provides an excellent example of how to walk with you in a loving relationship, communing with you and doing those things that are pleasing to you. Inform our minds with your Word, inspire our hearts through self-examination, and empower us with your Holy Spirit. In your Son's name and for our sake we make our petition known to you. Amen.*

Mimsie Robinson

A Brother Called Jabez

Jabez was honored more than his brothers; and his mother named him Jabez, saying, "Because I bore him in pain." Jabez called on the God of Israel, saying, "Oh that you would bless me and enlarge my border, and that your hand might be with me, and that you would keep me from hurt and harm!" And God granted what he asked. (1 Chronicles 4:9-10)

Because of the popular book of the same name, the prayer of Jabez has received a lot of attention from people of all walks of life over the past few years. As the gospel account reveals, Jabez was born to circumstances all too familiar to the average African American male. His mother was clearly unhappy about her son's birth. Instead of calling him a bundle of joy, she labeled him a bundle of pain. Was the pain alluded to by Jabez's mother merely the physical pain of childbirth? Was it the emotional pain caused by separation, divorce, or an unwanted pregnancy? Scripture does not give us a clear picture of the distressing circumstances that Jabez's mother confronted. However, the account of Jabez provides African American males with a model strategy for recovering our identity, discovering true prosperity, and leaving a good legacy despite the disappointing circumstances that surround us. From the Garden of Eden to the Garden of Gethsemane, Satan has been out to steal, kill, and destroy us by undermining these three critical areas of a man's life. Jesus came so that we "may have life, and have it abundantly" (John 10:10).

How do we overcome a broken identity? One of the deepest wounds a brother can experience can come from his earliest dealings with his parents, and Jabez had been given a name that reminded him of the rejection of his own mother. In the midst of hurt, Jabez discovered a truth that was also articulated by King David: "If my father and mother forsake me, the LORD will take me up" (Psalm 27:10). By God's grace, Jabez learned the power of faith. He did not focus on what people said about him, but concerned himself with what God thought of him. 1 Chronicles 4:9 says that Jabez had a reputation for being "honored more than his brothers." He was a descendant of the tribe of Judah, and the name Judah means "praise." He realized that we were made to praise God Almighty, who made us in his image (Genesis 1:26).

As men of African descent, many of us could argue that we have endured more assaults on our identity than any other group on the face of the earth. Our broken identity, caused by personal and societal injustice, must ultimately be healed by experiencing the living presence of our Wounded Healer, the Lord Jesus Christ. After experiencing new life in Christ (John 3:3; 2 Corinthians 5:17), we must allow God to help us develop a healthy understanding of ourselves by studying his Word and by cultivating a life of praise and sincere worship (John 4:24). God can redefine us in ways that no one else can.

Jabez understood the role of prayer in discovering true prosperity. In the prayer found in 1 Chronicles 4:10, Jabez nullifies the curses of his past. In spite of his onerous name, he cries out to God in pursuit of true blessings, a greater anointing upon his gifts, and the placement of God's mighty hand of guidance upon his daily life.

Have we brothers underestimated the power of prayer? It is not just a "sister thing." Prayer is what allows us to hold fast to our dreams, and dreams deferred become realities through prayer and persistence. Luke 18:1 says to "pray always and not to lose heart." Many of us have limited our prosperity through our impoverished prayer lives.

Finally, as African American men we should be concerned about our legacy. When our lives are full of God's blessings spiritually, relationally, and professionally, the end result will be a generational blessing that will lead to a powerful legacy of godliness and victorious living for our children and grandchildren. It is no wonder that the story of Jabez appears in a genealogy. The faithfulness of one brother like Jabez can reap a harvest of blessings in the lives of others for generations to come.

So let us not grow weary in doing what is right, for we will reap at harvest-time, if we do not give up. So then, whenever we have an opportunity, let us work for the good of all, and especially for those of the family of faith. (Galatians 6:9-10).

This is a blessing, indeed!

’ ’ ’

PRAYER: *Dear Lord, bless me and make me a blessing. Thank you for not allowing the labels of the past to affect my destiny. In the name of Jesus, I have a new identity, a guarantee of divine prosperity, and a wonderful legacy to leave to the generations that will come after me. For this I give you praise. Amen.*

Walter S. Thomas

THANK GOD FOR A SHEPHERD

The LORD is my shepherd, I shall not want. (Psalm 23:1)

There is no doubt in my mind that one of the hardest things for men to handle is the tremendous amount of responsibility that rests upon our shoulders. One of my preaching mentors used to remind me regularly that God had given us freedom, but with that freedom comes great responsibility. We must make sure the mortgage is paid, the utility bill is paid, the telephone is kept on, food is in the house, every child has what is needed, medical needs are met, and, on top of all that, that we are emotionally involved in the lives of our loved ones. This is a tall order, and often a thankless job. Many men do not feel as if they are given proper credit for what they try to accomplish. They feel that their actions are scrutinized and their efforts are minimized. Many a man has just gotten up and left because he could not handle the pressure. Some have turned to drugs or drink, while others have just given up on ever being truly happy and fulfilled.

It is in the hardest times that the words of David provide us with a breath of fresh air. Here is a young man who has the responsibility of caring for his master's sheep. This is no easy job; in fact, it is demanding. The sheep wander off, and they are attacked by marauding wild animals. They must be led to green pastures so that they will grow fat and wooly. So much rests upon the shepherd's shoulders; he is responsible if anything happens to even one of the sheep. It is with all of this in mind that the young David exclaims, "The LORD is my shepherd...." There is someone who is watching over David just as he is watching over the sheep. There is someone who is protective of David just as he is protective of the sheep.

Thank God we have a shepherd. There are many who depend upon us, but we can rest upon the Lord, for he is our shepherd. The beauty is in knowing what it means to be the Lord's; it means that "we shall not want."

, , ,

PRAYER: *Dear Lord, sometimes our responsibilities seem overwhelming, our tasks impossible to achieve. Take our hearts back to that still, calm, quiet stream. Bring healing to our troubled spirits. Remind us this day of what it means to not want for anything. Amen.*

Victor M. Davis

RESPONSIBILITY

The LORD God took the man and put him in the garden of Eden to till it and keep it. And the LORD God commanded the man, "You may freely eat of every tree of the garden; but of the tree of the knowledge of good and evil you shall not eat, for in the day that you eat of it you shall die." (Genesis 2:15-17)

The depth of our relationship with God depends on the level of responsibility to which we have remained faithful. We must respond to a given situation in a manner that displays reliability, as well as maturity and accountability that marks us as responsible. Responsible persons accept liability for the matters that have been entrusted to them.

We, as African American men, from the beginning of time have a responsibility to our God, families, communities, churches, and ourselves to "till and keep" that which God has entrusted to us. As we tend and watch over creation, we must realize the awesome and sacred trust that God has extended to man. African American men must recognize that when we fail to act in the best interest of our families and communities we are functioning outside of God's will, outside of his original plan for us "to have dominion" and to be responsible for those matters within our control.

Our responsibilities include care for our bodies, remaining health conscious and not submitting ourselves to the bondage of substance abuse and sexual promiscuity. It is our responsibility to be positive role models for the communities in which we reside and fellowship. We must be politically astute. Our families must know by our example that what we do is in the best interest of our wives and children. Most of all, we must exemplify the depth of our relationship with the Lord by making the proper moral and spiritual decisions that best reflect his character and command. To do this, African American men must assume the spiritual and personal practices of allowing God to use us in every aspect of our lives.

Brothers, we have been called to "till and keep the garden." Thus, we must be proactive in our efforts to live our lives as men of God. We can do all things through Christ who strengthens us (Philippians 4:13).

, , ,

PRAYER: *God, you created humanity in your image to do that which is pleasing in your sight. I need your Spirit to be with me in my actions so that I will be a good steward over all that you have entrusted to me. Thank you, Lord, for this awesome task, and may I forever be found in your favor. Amen.*

Gilbert H. Caldwell

A Letter to My Sons

Paul, an apostle of Christ Jesus by the command of God our Savior and of Christ Jesus our hope, To Timothy, my loyal child in the faith: Grace, mercy, and peace from God the Father and Christ Jesus our Lord. (1 Timothy 1:1–2)

Dear Dale and Paul,

My sons, I offer these words for your reflection.

Thank you for understanding my "calling" that pulled and pushed me to give my best energy and time to pastoral leadership in several churches. I know that I deprived you of some quality time that you deserved. Perhaps that is why, when you got older, you were unrelenting in "whipping" me on the basketball and tennis courts!

Thanks also for understanding why I felt called to be an insignificant participant in many of the struggles of the civil rights movement. In your childhood, I was away participating in "Freedom Summer" in Mississippi, involved in the Selma to Montgomery march, and the March on Washington. While you were at home with your mother, I was present with Dr. King when we challenged the lack of vision of the Boston School Committee. When you were ten and eight respectively, I experienced my first arrest in New York City, with Jesse Jackson and other pastors, as we blocked the offices of a major grocery chain over its hiring policies. Through all of this your mother and I sought to teach you something about this nation's gap between word and deed that made these efforts necessary. Thank you for understanding.

But, in recent years, Dale and Paul, you taught me to put my activism into perspective. You have an understanding of why it was necessary, but you reminded me—sometimes forcefully—that I do not serve this moment in history well by reminiscing excessively about the "good old days" of the movement. You gently remind me of the words in the hymn, "New occasions teach new duties." The twenty-first century, you tell me, does not need a replication of the old tactics, but it rather requires African Americans, particularly those of us who are middle class, to use our newly gained class status to close the class gap and to encourage a new level of parental and economic responsibility among our black sisters and brothers.

Dale and Paul, you have deepened my walk with God by understanding what I have tried to be and by teaching me to be relevant in the twenty-first century. Thank you!

With a love for you I am not ashamed to acknowledge,

Dad

, , ,

PRAYER: *God, you have been present with us in that unique relationship between father and sons. May we reflect the words of Christ: "Fathers and sons, learn from each other." Amen.*

William J. Key

≈≈≈

IN THE TIME
OF TROUBLE

*For he will hide me in his shelter in the day of trouble;
he will conceal me under the cover of his tent; he will
set me high on a rock. (Psalm 27:5)*

Young men yearn for their sixteenth birthday
and the rite of passage of driving, eventually
owning, and operating a car. Driving was so
important to me at that age; little did I know that
some of life's most challenging experiences
would take place behind the wheel.

Driving to and from Atlanta in the 1970s
with a friend, DeVerges Jones, I remembered our
fathers' insistence that we stay on the interstate
and be sensible. They had lived in the "old
South" and were acquainted with the unloving
ways of some who called it home. One night at
2:00 A.M. we found ourselves at an isolated, dark
tollbooth on Interstate 85 below Petersburg,
Virginia. As I was handing the toll taker fifteen
pennies and a dime, he glanced at our New York

tags, reached for his gun, and shouted, "Boy, give me a case quarter right now!"

Personal experiences, history lessons, and news accounts of racial trouble in the South informed my days. My prayer list grew even longer after this and other racially generated encounters. My carefree, teenage days were over, and I'd been thrust into a troubled world.

Some years later, while traveling home, I encountered slushy roads caused by a snow and ice storm. As I carefully fought to stay within the tracks of the preceding car, my vehicle gained speed, no longer moving at 30 miles an hour, but at 40, 45, 50, and faster. Approaching a familiar downgrade, I applied the brakes, but the car continued to accelerate. No matter how much I braked, nothing reduced the speed of my runaway vehicle. My prayer, as the car sped down the highway, was "Lord, help me!"

With my car out of control, I came to the realization that I was "in the valley" at that moment, but thanks be to God, I didn't have to stay there. In a matter of minutes I was at the base of a steep hill, and as my car climbed the hill, its speed diminished. I intermittently pumped the brakes, while my right hand pulled the emergency brake. Approaching the crest of the hill I shouted aloud, "Lord, have mercy on my soul!" A road sign read "Toll ahead." I prayed that the Lord would stop the car, and I knew that he had heard me and would answer my prayer. The car came to a stop just a few feet from the toll booth.

More recently, I again drove down I-85 south of Petersburg, this time increasingly aware of my 1970 2:00 A.M. encounter with the toll taker. I became uneasy, wondering what would happen when I pulled up to the booth where the gun-toting toll taker had made his presence known. Once again, I called on the Lord for help, and as quickly as the uneasiness had overtaken me, it was gone. Much to my surprise, not only was my discomfort gone, but so was the toll booth!

The Lord has continued to bless my life by answering prayers. I know there will always be valleys, as well as upside and downside mountain experiences, but I'm determined to rejoice and give thanks to the Lord for all his blessings.

, , ,

ON THIS DAY: *I will continue to give God praise, because I know the Lord will provide whatever I need.*

Rayshad A. Holmes

≋

I'VE GOT ME TOGETHER

In all these things we are more than conquerors
through him who loved us.
(Romans 8:37)

Stop worrying.
Stop complaining.
Stop. I've got me together.

My credit is bad, but that hasn't stopped me.
I have lost one or two jobs, but that too hasn't
   stopped me.
And yes, higher education came in the form of
   Streets 101, but that hasn't stopped me either.
I've got me together.

I have tried to be better than my father was, to do
   more for my children than he did for me.
I have tried to break the generational curse that
   runs so deep and can destroy so much.
I have planned for a future not dependent upon
   material possessions

———

And planted in fertile soil where crops of principle, ethics, and hard work are readily available.

My appearance demands respect. I don't tamper with plaits, gold teeth, or the like.

I stand assured that I am, I can, and I will.

I see more than television, and I understand more than the obvious.

Yep, I've got me together.

I realize that in order to play this game, I need something more than a record deal, a drug operation, or a couple of boys to help me get my idea up off the ground.

I know that battling life against "the man" is some fantasy most people use as an excuse for their shortcomings and failure to face reality.

But not me.

I've got me together.

I have fortified myself by having a relationship with God that supercedes persons, places, and things.

I have surrounded myself with people from whom I can glean inspiration each day.

I stimulate my mind by reading, writing, and walking boldly through doors that once read "No Coloreds Allowed."

And yes, I see myself as more than….

More than a social security number, more than a crime statistic, more than a conqueror, and more than just another one.

I've got me together.

So if my ability to do this highlights your inability to regard and respect me as such,

Then we'll simply have to part ways.

Because when you've been where I've been, seen what I've seen, and done some of the things I've had to do just to survive,

Satisfying others at the risk of humiliating yourself is not an option.

I told you before,

I've got me together,

But I can't assume responsibility for you.

> > >

PRAYER: *I've got me together, Lord. Guide me. By your grace, keep me together. Amen.*

Oscar Crawford

≈≈≈

BREATHE

"Be still, and know that I am God!"
(Psalm 46:10)

I love people. I adore people. I need people. But, every now and then, people get on my last nerve, frustrate me to no end, and make me wish they would all just go away. I know this never happens to you, right? Right.

When I find myself in that kind of mood, I realize I am caught up in my own frustration. In that moment, I am angry and feel like I am broadcasting evil energy. My stress level is way up and if I don't get help soon, I feel like I am going to explode.

When I get like this, I go to two really good friends. Both love me unconditionally. Neither one of them is human.

When I have had all that I can manage and when I want—no, need—to get away from people before I say or do something stupid, I go home. I get with Sooki (Soo-kee), our beautiful

Lhasa Apso, and I get with the Creator. I ask Sooki to take me for a walk, and as we walk, I listen and wait for the Creator's voice to speak to my present situation.

That process of walking, listening, and waiting involves these five steps that never fail to restore me to mental health and spiritual peace.

1. When you find yourself in turmoil, knocked off your emotional feet, position yourself *(breathe)* in a quiet, internal stillness where you can listen.

2. Do not be in a hurry *(breathe)*. You didn't get to this emotional state in a moment. Be in the stillness until you can stand on your emotional feet again.

3. When you have reached your emotional feet again *(breathe)*, do a 360-degree review of your spiritual, physical, social, and emotional environment.

4. Determine what your multiple environments need. If you determine you possess what is needed *(breathe)*, offer it. Remember, you cannot give what you do not possess.

5. If you do not possess what is needed, a courageous act awaits you *(breathe)*. Find an

environment more suitable to what you have to offer.

When I have walked with Sooki and my Creator long enough, often I cannot recall what prompted my previous condition. These five action steps work because they are premised upon everlasting principle: "Be still and know...."

, , ,

PRAYER: *Lord, help me to breathe, so I may be proactively still more often. Amen.*

LeDelvin J. Peavy

≈≈≈

KEEP GOD IN YOUR GOALS

In my Father's house there are many dwelling places. If it were not so, would I have told you that I go to prepare a place for you? (John 14:2)

While growing up, I became devoted to the "American dream." I often read magazines that showcased the finer things in life, making myself familiar with the names of expensive automobiles and jewelry. My intentions were to do well in school, graduate from college, and earn a great position with a Fortune 500 company that would enable me to afford all the worldly possessions of which I had so long dreamt.

With a B.S. in business under my belt, off I went to set the world on fire. My first position out of college was with a Fortune 500 company, and though it was an entry-level position, my confidence never wavered. I knew that my ambition and hard work would take me straight up the corporate ladder. I soon learned, however, that although companies often speak of opportunities for advancement during interviews, they rarely make good on those promises. I have never been one to use the race card, but I learned that race does become a factor in corporate America.

Not to be discouraged, I left the Fortune 500 company and began working for an even larger company, this time Fortune 200. Sadly, I soon learned that the same problem existed within the new company. The opportunities to advance were limited, unless I wanted to be a team leader, which was another name for overseer. Chances to break into the marketing or sales departments simply didn't exist, and the few opportunities that did present themselves were often handed to someone in advance, before the positions had even been posted.

These negative experiences caused my faith in the American dream to waver, and that's when the Lord stepped in and showed me that in order to be truly successful, my devotion to and faith in God needed to be in place. I had been serving corporate gods in search of worldly things, but Jesus reminded me that service to him reaps the greatest reward of all.

The Bible says in John 14:2, "In my Father's house there are many dwelling places. If it were not so, would I have told you that I go to prepare a place for you?" It used to make me proud to work under a big company's name until I realized that the Lord holds the greatest title of all. Since that realization, I have achieved success in both my professional and personal life. There's nothing wrong with having goals, but I've learned that for true success you must have Jesus leading you on the path.

, , ,

ON THIS DAY: *I pray for guidance that I might serve as an example of a strong Christian man.*

Michael Brown

FROM "ORDINARY" TO "EXTRAORDINARY"

He responded, "But sir, how can I deliver Israel? My clan is the weakest in Manasseh, and I am the least in my family." The LORD said to him, "But I will be with you,..." (Judges 6:15-16)

When the phone rang, I had never been so anxious to talk to my brother. Even when he had been in the U.S. Navy, catching jets in the Pacific for six years, I hadn't before been so eager to hear his voice. David had just lived every middle-aged man's nightmare: he had spent a weekend in Chicago's notorious Cook County Jail.

Married and the father of two sons, David had been stopped the previous Saturday for a minor traffic violation and a computer check revealed an old traffic warrant. He was unable to go before a judge until Monday afternoon, and his family, fearing the worst, prayed for his safety.

Hearing his voice on the phone was the answer to our prayers. David told me how he had spent the first night cold and hungry in the police lockup. Overnight, the police brought in a young brother with heavily bandaged wrists, who was obviously distraught and sobbing quietly. David began to converse with him and found out he had attempted suicide earlier in the evening. The young man had just found out that his only daughter had died of Sudden Infant Death Syndrome, and he had learned this news while in the lockup. He blamed himself, believing that if he had not been in custody, he would have somehow saved his daughter.

David spent that night offering the only comfort he could: he explained that the man's daughter was wrapped in the loving arms of our Savior and that no one's actions could have changed what happened. Eventually David got the young man to recognize and accept that we should not put a question mark where God has placed a period.

The next day, when they were transferred to the Cook County Jail, the young man introduced David to his gang leader, explaining to the other man how my brother had comforted him. In this alien, stressful environment, the gang leader offered David protection and gave him a primer on survival: where to stand, where to look (and not to look), what to say, etc. Word quickly spread of David's deed, and soon gang members by the dozens came to seek his advice on education, the military, children, and life in general. David hadn't realized how thirsty these men were for wisdom and how infrequent their contact was with a man who wasn't judgmental or trying to exploit them, their mothers, or their children. While the time he spent in that jail was harrowing, David told me he had also found it rewarding.

One thing puzzled him: Why was it so easy to interact with such men behind bars, when "on the street" he didn't think he could get the time of day without winding up in the hospital? But I felt he was there, not under the protection of the gang, but under God's protection. The Bible is filled with examples of otherwise "ordinary" men doing God's work. Two common features are clear in such events. First, these "ordinary" men find themselves in places not of their choosing, and second, God's work seems impossible to do until those men rely upon the

Lord for strength and salvation. The transformation from the "ordinary" to the "extraordinary" comes from God. The opportunities for such transforming ministry are no less plentiful now than they were in biblical times; we are just often unaware that it is God's hand that guides and protects us, no matter where we go.

, , ,

PRAYER: *Mighty God, attune my spirit to the work of your guiding and protecting hand today, that I might seize any opportunity to let you transform me from the ordinary to the extraordinary in service to your people. Amen.*

William Miner

IN THE REALM OF REDEMPTION

In creation we see God's hand. In redemption we see his heart. (Anonymous)

Redemption is of God, and it requires our genuine commitment and total involvement. We are asked only to believe, thereby making ourselves available to be converted, delivered, rescued, restored, and set free—in a word, redeemed. We do not have to amend, buy back, pay off, or trade in anything. Christ's death has done it all for us.

Then why is redemption so difficult for us to obtain and sustain, more difficult than other functions of the Trinity? Reconciliation, for example, seems to be more accessible. We often "come to terms" in our relationships with others—even with God. We "do good." We follow the rules. Take mercy and justice for example. We can be big-hearted. We may even go out of our way to help someone else because it gives us such a good feeling about ourselves and about humanity. So why is redemption so hard?

Jan Johnson, in *Discipleship Journal* (vol. 21, no. 1, pp. 56-60) used a well known "good deed" to demonstrate how redemption might be invoked. When thinking about feeding the homeless at holiday time, two choices often come to mind: making a donation and staying home for a fun dinner with the family, or going to a homeless shelter and helping serve the meal. Johnson suggests a third choice: inviting that homeless person who inhabits the steps outside your church or office building into your home for dinner.

Reconciliation? No problem! Send a donation. Contribute to the NAACP or the Urban League. Attend the annual MLK breakfast. Participate in a joint worship service with a neighboring congregation of a different ethnicity.

Mercy and justice? No problem! Serve meals at a homeless shelter. Deliver food baskets at Thanksgiving or Christmas. Solicit for the Cancer Fund or the United Way.

And redemption? Invite a homeless person to your holiday dinner. Become a Big Brother or

Sister. Tutor inner city children. Train people to become financially literate. Volunteer at an AIDS clinic or hospice.

Look again when you think there are only two choices. There might be a third choice, one that will take you into the realm of redemption.

, , ,

PRAYER: *Challenge me this day, O Lord, to move beyond my comfort zone. Test the limits of my creativity, of my commitment, of my love for your children. Amen.*

Campbell B. Singleton III

≋

GUARD YOUR HEARTS

Keep your heart with all vigilance, for from it flow the springs of life. (Proverbs 4:23)

Am I capable of this? This sobering question came to mind as I looked upon the massive collapse of tons of steel and the cruel destruction of thousands of human lives at Ground Zero in September of 2001. It was a surreal moment as I ostensibly peered in the mirror at myself and observed the reflection of human nature. The penetrating truth is that each of us has the capacity to inflict great pain upon others when we allow seeds of hatred, envy, selfishness, greed, and lust to fester in our hearts.

The unspeakable tragedy at the World Trade Center sounded a global clarion call for people to become introspective and fight the wars within and without. A national alarm is ringing, calling us to rise out of smoldering ashes and billows of smoke to confess mistakes and repent from deeds that have provoked hatred and afflicted pain. A trumpet blast has boomed, summoning black men to guard their hearts and cease participation in homicide and suicide in the face of genocide.

At Ground Zero, the worst of humanity and the best of humanity were present in the same debacle. The worst of humanity violently disrupted our lives and caused us deep grief. The worst of humanity cared not about the profound bonds of love that inextricably connected one to another. The worst of humanity ruthlessly attacked when our backs were turned, and shamelessly celebrated our recurring nightmare.

Conversely, the best of humanity rolled up their sleeves and sought to rescue survivors and recover valuables. The best of humanity tirelessly and unselfishly worked to the highest degree to save, deliver, and heal broken people in a shattered world. The best of humanity demonstrated the nature of God and gave without reservation. The best of humanity showed compassion for the vulnerable. I praised God in that valley, for God does dwell where shadows of death linger.

Many are asking, "How can we help?" Brothers, don't let hurt turn into hate, nor anger into vengeance and violence, but guard your hearts, for out of the heart flows life.

, , ,

PRAYER: *O God, create in us a clean heart and renew in us a right spirit. Amen.*

John E. Jackson Sr.

The Battle Is the Lord's

But David said to the Philistine, "You come to me with sword and spear and javelin; but I come to you in the name of the LORD of hosts, the God of the armies of Israel, whom you have defied. This very day the LORD will deliver you into my hand, and I will strike you down and cut off your head; and I will give the dead bodies of the Philistine army this very day to the birds of the air and to the wild animals of the earth, so that all the earth may know that there is a God in Israel, and that all this assembly may know that the LORD does not save by sword and spear; for the battle is the LORD's and he will give you into our hand." (1 Samuel 17:41-47)

The scene in which the youthful David stands before the seasoned warrior and giant Goliath has always caused my very soul to tremble. The words David spoke make my soul come to attention: "You come to me with sword and spear and javelin; but I come to you in the name of the LORD of hosts, the God of the armies of Israel, whom you have defied."

55

My church's theme for the year of 2001 was, "We are God's people." Reflecting on the story of David and my church's theme puts steel in my back. To say we belong to God is a sobering acknowledgment. There is no other affiliation in life than can deliver the promise of eternity. If we believe God is all-powerful and that Christ rose from the grave to sit at God's right hand in glory, then no event in life can eclipse the lasting hope of joining him there some day.

The same God who called the stars out to shine, the same God who by speaking caused light to streak forth from stygian darkness, the same God who stood up one Sunday morning having turned back the powers of hell, is responsible for us. Therefore, as the young David proclaimed, "It is not by sword or by spear that the LORD saves, for the battle is the LORD's." There will be many things in life that will threaten you, and many shadows of uncertainty will fall on you, but you will not stand alone, because there is one greater who holds us in his mighty hand.

My brothers, listen to one who knew the pain of unguided churchmen. Listen to one who was familiar with family disappointment and letdowns. Listen to the Rev. Charles Tindley put that pain in perspective: "Harder yet may be the fight; right may often yield to might; wickedness a while may reign; Satan's cause may seem to gain. There is a God that rules above with hands of mighty power and a heart of love. If I am right, he'll fight my battle, and I shall have peace someday!" Give yourselves, my brothers, to the Word and to the presence of Jesus, for we fight on the Lord's side today.

, , ,

PRAYER: *Lord God almighty, remind us in our souls that we belong to you. Remove our fear, frustration, and doubt. Bless us with strength, pride, and faith to carry on as you would have us do each day. Amen.*

Ralph W. Holmes

≈

RICH RECOLLECTIONS OF A FRIENDSHIP

A friend loves at all times, and kinsfolk are born to share adversity. (Proverbs 17:17)

September 15, 1999 was a memorable day in my life, for it was on that day that I had to bid farewell to a lifelong friend when he passed away. I have many memories from the association Deacon John F. White Sr. and I had over forty years of friendship, and on the day of John's death, my mind raced back to the early days of our association, which was spiritually based and nurtured by our faith in God and our activities at the 19th Street Baptist Church in South Philadelphia. It was there that John and I labored in Sunday school, the young adult choir, and Baptist Training Union services. I was privileged to serve as worship leader, while John rendered music on the piano in addition to leading many training sessions for those who were in attendance.

Many manifestations of the power of God and his blessings were shown during our Baptist Training Union sessions. Foremost in my memories were the occasional visits to our services by Rev. William Augustus Jones and Rev. Harold Carter, both of whom were students at the time at Crozier Theological Seminary in Chester, Pennsylvania. John and I would never forget the fine contributions the two pastors and friends made to the success and memories of our "work in the vineyard."

How well do I recollect the Sunday morning services at 19th St. Baptist, particularly the second Sunday of each month when the young adult choir provided the music. John and I were members of the choir; he sang baritone and I sang bass. One of our favorite selections was "Since I Met Jesus." The lyrics were enthralling, and we both strove to live out the affirmations in the song.

It is so rewarding to recollect the many years John and I were blessed by God to "work out our soul salvation," acknowledging always that all our good and perfect gifts came from God. The Lord did great things for us for which we were glad. One of John's favorite sayings that I shall always remember was, "The life of service is the life that counts, and blessed is the man that finds his joy in lifting the burdens of others."

Yes, my dear friend "ran his race" and kept the faith, and while I still experience moments of sadness over his untimely departure, I glory in the fact that, because of our unity in Christ, I will see him again, at that place God has prepared for all his people before the foundation of the earth.

, , ,

PRAYER: *Dear Lord, the memories of family and friends who have gone on to be with you remain fresh. Their influences remain long after their passing. May I live my life in such a way that my influences will be remembered and valued until that day when all your saints are reunited. Amen.*

Lawrence Hargrave

≈≈

PASS IT ON

And observe those who live according to the example you have in us. (Philippians 3:17)

I am a witness that we stand on the shoulders of those who have gone before us. Consequently, I am thankful for those elders and forbears who have had a positive impact on my life and touched me in ways that have helped define who I am.

The following individuals are among those who by example influenced my life. In my youth, Rev. Seward was an example of a dynamic young minister. Over 32 years ago, Deacon Poole gave me profound words of advice as I left my home community to begin a new career. Rev. Porter, a childhood friend of my mother and now a valued friend and colleague of mine, taught music to my Uncle Jimmie and Aunt Carol, and they both passed their appreciation of music on to me. Coach Shaper showed my high school basketball team how the last place "doormats" could, through discipline, determination, and perseverance, become competitive challengers in one year and champions in two. Mrs. Alexander exposed me to the idea of lifelong learning when she returned to school to receive her college degree.

I have, over the past few years, been able to seek out some of those who were influential during my formative years and to at least say, "Thank you." While many times we are able to do this with immediate family, sometimes life's changes and personal circumstances remove us from the spheres of influence of others who impacted our lives, and we are unable to tell them what they have meant to us.

While we may not be able to thank those persons, we are obligated to pass on to successive generations the faith and values that we have inherited from them. I count it an added blessing when a young person suggests to me that something that I did, perhaps unknowingly, stuck with them and had a positive impact. In the words of Jesus as recorded by Luke, "From everyone to whom much has been given, much will be required; and from the one to whom much has been entrusted, even more will be demanded" (Luke 12:48).

We are required to pass it on. Our values, our ethics, our culture, and our faith. Pass it on.

, , ,

PRAYER: *I pray that on this day I might find an opportunity to pass it on. Amen.*

Donald Young

≈≈≈

HANDLING THOSE
BAD FEELINGS

I lift up my eyes to the hills—from where will my help come? My help comes from the LORD, who made heaven and earth. (Psalm 121:1-2)

We all experience disappointment in life. One great disappointment in my life was the lack of a complete family. In my childhood community, father figures were not common, and I myself did not have a father in my life. This sometimes caused me to have unhealthy and confused feelings. It was an issue powerful enough to cause me to question my existence, even as a child.

Much later in life, mixed feelings of hurt, distress, guilt, and shame over my lack of a father resurfaced. I had no idea that those feelings would haunt me so much later in life. I thought that if I had a father around, life would have been different, better. Sometimes the wounds and suffering would linger so long that I often believed that I myself was a mistake.

The fact is that those feelings were real, and I needed to deal with them. My personal relationship with the Lord helped me immensely as I faced my emotions. I would often find myself seeking refuge in the Lord and being massaged by his mercy, grace, and peace. God is so awesome that he even sent others into my life to help alleviate and vanquish those bad feelings. He replaced the bad feelings with love, peace, and joy. I can truly appreciate what God has done for me, knowing that I could trust him made the outcome a miracle.

African Americans have never known what it means to have an easy way of life. We are not guaranteed a trouble-free life, but through Jesus Christ we have access to a peace that passes all understanding. When emotional times creep up on us, let us let go and be pampered by God's remarkable passion.

, , ,

PRAYER: *In times of turmoil, O God, please hide me in your bosom. When I am approached by unresolved feelings of distress or dismay, grant peace to my commotion. Amen.*

Ed Bowman

Faithful through the Valley

For surely I know the plans I have for you, says the LORD, plans for your welfare and not for harm, to give you a future with hope. (Jeremiah 29:11)

Is it night or day? If I conclude that it is night, I empower the adversary. Negative thoughts move in and cloud the mind. My night view is one that sees only that I have a job that does not pay benefits, and how difficult it is for an African American male in his late 50s to find a good position in the work force. When I focus on such things, the world seems dark, indeed.

If I count my blessings, I see daylight. I have a loving wife of thirty-two years, our health, and a supportive church family. I am finding contract work that is sufficient to pay all of our bills each month. My wife is not forced to work; she can be a fulltime parent to the five-year-old great-nephew we are raising. And above all, I have peace.

I choose to use idle time to count my blessings. There is no incentive to focus on my challenges. One's mental health is maintained by following the advice of the apostle Paul, who wrote in Philippians 4:8: "…if there is anything worthy of praise, think about these things."

It is in this positive frame of mind that I choose to be faithful. I have complete confidence that if I continue to praise, pray, work in my ministry, tithe, read, and study the Word; meet with the men's cell group for Bible study, discussion, and prayer; and be present in church each Sunday to hear an inspired message, God will continue to bless my life. I remain assured that everything is OK with my life in God's gentle and capable hands.

God's guidance and peace are greater than any material blessing. It is his grace and mercy that sustain me. It is the light of his love that shortens the night, levels the valley, and allows me to praise him every day.

, , ,

PRAYER: *Gracious and all-wise God, we give thanks to you for your love, grace, and mercy. We thank you for the gift of family and church and for their* prayers. You have a purpose for our lives and have provided us gifts for the building of your kingdom. Now help us to be open to your will and mindful of your blessings. We offer this prayer and this meditation in your name. Amen.

Henry P. Davis III

≋

ALL THINGS ARE POSSIBLE

For your Father knows what you need before you ask him. (Matthew 6:8)

I have always listened with deep interest to the testimonies of saints who testified that they could hear the Lord speaking to them through the voice of a lost parent. As a young boy, before I understood the wonder of the spiritual voice, I thought the saints heard actual voices. In those testimonies I could hear the Word of God in action.

Today I hear many young people blame their failures on not having a parent, or on having an absentee parent. The reality is that African Americans were more parentless in slavery than they are today. How was it that African Americans were able to rise up out of slavery to achieve so much when many were severed from any kind of loving relationship? The answer is God. Pick up any collection of slave narratives and you can read about the divine direction that guided each and every step of the displaced African people. It was during this time that the slaves came to know Jesus as a mother to the motherless and a father to the fatherless.

Today we do not face anything more impossible than what our foreparents faced when they rose up out of slavery, or when the Israelites, led by Moses, departed from Egypt. With God all things are possible. But when we refuse to listen to the voice of the heavenly Father, the possible becomes impossible. The voice of God our Father that guided our foreparents, can guide us each today.

Not only does our heavenly Father want to see us grow and develop to enhance his kingdom, but we are also called to be like a father to those in need of fathering. It is easy for us to see ourselves as sons needing a parent, but we are also called to father those who need reconciliation, forgiveness, and love. It is easy to identify with the wanderings of the prodigal son, but true growth in Christ is realized when we can identify with the father of the prodigal son. In the same way this father continued to love his son when he followed after his own desires, we too must realize that God has empowered us to be earthly fathers in our present world. Every day we must listen to the voice of our heavenly Father and extend love to those without.

, , ,

PRAYER: *Our Father, I stretch my hand to you, asking that you would strengthen me to stretch my other hand to lift and to love those who are in need. Thank you for divine guidance. I pray that others would see you through me. Amen.*

Wayne E. Croft Sr.

REST

But he himself went a day's journey into the wilderness, and came and sat down under a solitary broom tree. He asked that he might die: "It is enough; now, O LORD, take away my life, for I am no better than my ancestors." (1 Kings 19:4)

On October 7, 2001, our church dedicated its new million-dollar, multipurpose building, which is known as Redeemer Christian Life and Education Center. It was an exciting occasion, a day many of us will never forget—especially me. Four years ago, this day was envisioned as only a dream. The committee and I worked tirelessly to achieve that dream. I prayed, cried, preached, and invested energy and time to see this project come to fruition. The time had come to celebrate. The choir processed into the sanctuary singing one of the great hymns of the church, "The Church's One Foundation." Scripture from the Old and New Testaments were read; prayer was offered to God; a statement of purpose was delivered, and the choir sang one of my favorite hymns, "Glory to His Name." It was a high and holy moment. Something, however, happened to me. While everyone was singing "Glory to His Name," I was sobbing. It hit me unexpectedly. I should have been rejoicing, but I was crying. These were not tears of joy but the tears of heaviness. I was tired, weary, and worn.

In the midst of the singing, I began to think about all the work I personally had put into this project—the running back and forth to City Hall, the hurdles overcome when the bank approved us for the loan but took almost a year to give us the money, and the voices that said this could not be done. The dream had been fulfilled, but a burden rested heavily upon my shoulders. Like the prophet Elijah, I felt like crying out, "Enough, Lord!" I should have been rejoicing, but I was under a broom tree ready to throw up my hands.

All human beings have three gauges that we must check. We have spiritual, physical, and emotional gauges. Elijah had the same. However, he had drained himself spiritually on

Mount Carmel fighting the false prophets of Baal. He had drained himself physically running more than fifty miles from Jezebel, and he had drained himself emotionally thinking about Jezebel's vow to see him dead within twenty-four hours. Elijah neglected to check his gauges, and so he found himself running on empty, sputtering to a halt under a broom tree and wishing for death.

We ought to take one day out of each week to rest and check our three gauges. If not, when we should be rejoicing we will be sighing, out of gas under a broom tree.

, , ,

ON THIS DAY: *I will commit myself to one sabbath day each week so that I may be effectively used of God for the rest of the week.*

Howard O. King Sr.

≋

YOU, TOO,
CAN OVERCOME

A slack hand causes poverty, but the hand of the diligent makes rich. A child who gathers in summer is prudent, but a child who sleeps in harvest brings shame. (Proverbs 10:4-5)

It has been said, "If I had known then what I know now...wow!" Maybe if more men with "know how" had taken the time to pass it on, those of my generation would have avoided some of the inevitable pitfalls of life.

Being an African American male in this society means bearing special burdens, most of them imposed by people who single us out because of the color of our skin and the texture of our hair. As long as each generation of black males is required to start at "square one," they are going to find themselves bogged down, and many will fall by the wayside before they reach the point of surviving and competing at a level that signifies success.

As one who started life's journey somewhere below "square one," I feel that I can pass on words that will motivate and give hope to those who despair. I learned early in life that "luck works best for those who are not dependent on it," and that hard work and good work habits are copartners with luck. Fatherless at the age of ten and a ninth-grade dropout at thirteen, I began serious work in my hometown, Pensacola, Florida, in February 1939. Every aspect of African American life at that time was thoroughly segregated. Black males who attempted to fight the system were "black-balled" in the workplace. Bodily harm was commonplace; death quite frequent.

For three years I held several mediocre jobs: working on an ice truck, as a delivery boy for a grocery store and a drug store, as a janitor, and as a waiter. Forty-two years later I retired from a federal agency in Washington, D.C., where I had been deputy director of a significant program, a position that made and influenced many important decisions. The road from where I'd begun to where I ended up had many turns and quite a few detours, but determination to succeed helped me to use the obstacles I encountered as stepping stones.

Two decisions that I made early in life made the difference for me. First, I realized that education is an equalizer. Twelve-and-a-half years after dropping out of high school, I returned to school. By May 1956, I had fulfilled the requirements for a B.S. in business and economics from Florida A & M University.

Second, I was steadfast in my faith. When plans failed to produce as anticipated, I always concluded, "God does not want me to move in that direction; I am better off without it."

Although I worked two jobs and attended school at the same time, I always made time for church and community activities, as I was convinced that a "balanced" life is a more productive one. I urge my younger brothers to take to heart what I have learned: that having faith that God will help us and taking steps to improve ourselves are two sides of the same coin.

, , ,

PRAYER: *Heavenly Father, others throughout history have learned to overcome. Give us the patience, courage, and perseverance to do the same. Amen.*

Kent L. Poindexter

≋

ARE YOU TRULY FREE?

For freedom Christ has set us free. Stand firm, therefore, and do not submit again to a yoke of slavery. (Galatians 5:1)

The reality of being black in America is that we will be considered less than perfect because of our skin color and other features. America has taught us that coarse hair, thick lips, and dark skin make African Americans ugly and inferior, and this "brainwashing" has had far-reaching effects on us. Current styles of dress, though they defy white culture, are actually patterned after clothing worn by inmates. Our children, donning these clothes, say they are "keepin' it real." Somehow, we have been convinced that being uneducated, living in substandard housing, and destroying one another is "keepin' it real." As an old deacon once said, "We's loose, but we ain't free!"

What is freedom? The dictionary says that it is independence, liberation, and privilege. It is the right to choose the direction of our lives without allowing society to negatively influence us. Freedom is escape from the stereotypes that keep us shackled to less than the best.

The apostle Paul speaks of these negative influences in his letter to the Galatians, a Christian community seeking freedom from the influences of paganism. Paul says that God, through Jesus Christ, has called us to freedom from the shackles of this world. The message of Jesus Christ is a message of freedom to those who have been disenfranchised, oppressed, and abused. Jesus tells us God doesn't care about our social status, our education, our color, or anything else that might matter to the world. We are special simply because we are children of God. No one is excluded from God's love or the freedom to be what God created us to be. We were not born to be shackled by the teachings and expectations of those who want to dominate us. God's love means that we are indeed free.

, , ,

PRAYER: *God, when we are shackled by heavy burdens, help us to remember that in Christ we can be free. Amen.*

Marvin A. McMickle

≈≈≈

A TRANSFORMED LIFE

Paul, an apostle of Christ Jesus by the will of God. (Ephesians 1:1)

When Paul introduced himself in his letter to the church at Ephesus, he made reference only to his role as an apostle of Jesus Christ. However, Paul had not always been an apostle. There was a time in his life when he was Saul, an enemy and antagonist of Jesus Christ. Paul had not always been on the Lord's side, but by the will of God, his life was transformed so that God could use him for a different purpose.

I suspect that Saul was not alone in the process of transformation. In fact, I would suggest that most of us who are now numbered among the disciples of Jesus once lived through a period of rebellion, resistance, and recklessness. My own path into full-time Christian service was anything but a straight route, and I would not be surprised if many of the men who now occupy the pulpits and the pews of our churches across the country have had similar experiences of transformation.

Today I am the pastor of a large Baptist church, a tenured seminary professor with a Ph.D., and an author of several books. Thirty-five years ago, I was a hoodlum, a gang-banger, and a near alcoholic. My life was so far off track that a member of my home church in Chicago took me for a ride in his car and stopped in front of Cook County Jail. As we sat there talking, he told me that if I did not change how I was living my life, I would most likely find myself inside those prison walls. That man shocked me into reality and opened my ears to hear the gospel for the first time.

Today, like Paul, I am an unlikely servant in the work of kingdom-building, and two things are crystal clear to me. First, like Paul, most of us have come to Christ after having wallowed and wasted a portion of our lives in riotous living (Luke 15:13). We need to celebrate the transformation that Christ has made within us. Second, there are younger men who need somebody to care about them like that man in Chicago cared about me. Rather than criticizing and condemning the younger brothers of our communities, perhaps we need to help them see and bring forth the untapped potential within them.

, , ,

PRAYER: *Lord, thank you for giving me a second chance at life and the opportunity to work for your kingdom. Help me to remember the older brothers within my community who worked to salvage my life when I seemed determined to follow a path of self-destruction. Give me the determination to do for others what was once done for me. Amen.*

Keith W. Roberson

THE GREATEST SHIP OF ALL

Therefore confess your sins to one another, and pray for one another, so that you may be healed. The prayer of the righteous is powerful and effective. (James 5:16)

As I look back over my pastoral ministry and my twenty-year walk with the Lord, I truly thank God for *koinonia*. The gift of fellowship is one of the greatest gifts that anyone can have, and, best of all, it's available to anyone who truly wants to receive it.

I am blessed to have gone through much of life with a few fellows whom I consider my true friends. The Lord has fixed it so that we are all married with children, and we are all pastors. I am blessed to know that I can call on them morning, noon, or night to talk, knowing that what is said will stay between us.

Unfortunately, too many men are looking to become great leaders for God yet do not realize that one of our purposes on earth is to share God's love with others (John 13:34). One of the differences between men and women is the fact that women need physical, tangible fellowship for strength. Men tend to hibernate, to go off by themselves to deal with their problems. We should take a page out of our sisters' book and learn that the body of Christ is intended for *koinonia*, physical fellowship.

True liberty comes when you can let yourself go with your brother and share and be blessed. After all, the Lord has set that brother aside to be your friend and confidant. We are reminded through the Word that our vertical relationship (our relationship with God) has everything to do with our horizontal relationship (our relationship with others) (John 13:35).

I break bread with my good friends almost every Tuesday, and we discuss our walk with the Lord, our ministry, and human relationships. We share our weaknesses, and we pray with one another. The weeks that I don't meet with them is when I realize how blessed I am to be on the greatest ship of all, the "Ship of Fellowship."

As we allow our flesh to die and as we realize that we have been taught some bogus, macho nonsense about "being a man" and handling problems alone, we will be able to get in touch with our real spiritual man. We will understand that we are our brothers' keeper, and that we must encourage each other and restore anyone who has been overtaken with a fault. We cannot fulfill James 5:16 unless we board the ship of fellowship with Jesus and our fellow man.

, , ,

PRAYER: *Dear Lord, you created us as unique individuals, but we are meant to live in community, to share one another's blessings and joys, as well as their tears and sorrows. Help me to be the same source of comfort, support, and inspiration that other brothers have been to me. Amen.*

≋

DRY SPELL

Why are you cast down, O my soul, and why are you disquieted within me? Hope in God; for I shall again praise him, my help…" (Psalm 42:5)

Have you ever prayed and felt like God would not answer? Two years ago, I was on vacation and, as usual, I was awake at 5:00 A.M. for early morning prayer. My prayer that day was for the needs of my family, for difficulties they were going through at the time. As I was praying, my inner feelings just didn't seem right. I felt that I was not connecting with God, and that my words were just beating the air. The more I prayed, the more it felt like God wasn't hearing me, but I knew that wasn't true.

My circumstances seemed to overwhelm me and increased my need to hear from God. I knew I needed to keep praying, that if I stopped praying, I would spiritually die. As a man in a desert needs water, my heart, my soul, and my spirit desperately needed to hear from God. I don't fully understand why I experienced the dry spell, but I do know it was part of God's plan, because it made me even more determined to keep right on praying.

Suddenly, a Scripture came to me: "Why are you cast down, O my soul, and why are you disquieted within me? Hope in God; for I shall again praise him, my help..." (Psalm 42:5). As the words traveled through my heart, I could feel the comfort of the Holy Spirit engulfing me. Oh, it's a good thing when the comfort of the Lord comes to us!

I remember reading Psalm 42:1–2. The passage speaks about David's thirst for feeling God's nearness. Sometimes during our own prayer times we may feel the same emptiness, which I call a dry spell. When you encounter the feeling, keep right on praying, for Psalm 34:15 tells us that "The eyes of the LORD are on the righteous, and his ears are open to their cry." So keep right on praying, brother. Pray until the Lord showers your dry spell with his richest blessings.

, , ,

PRAYER: *Father God, in your Word you said that when we pray, we should believe that you have heard* *our prayer. Help us to remember that you will answer, and that you will supply all of our needs according to your riches in glory by Christ Jesus. Amen.*

Jarrett Phillip Coger

≋

THE NUTRITIONAL MEAL

The wise lay up knowledge, but the babbling of a fool brings ruin near. (Proverbs 10:14)

Many struggles come with being a young black Christian male, but as a man of Christ I have attempted to work through the temptations and times of pain with God walking alongside. I have been blessed to learn so many lessons inside my church home, a community that leads and guides me in almost everything I do. The church is a place for worshipping our Creator, but it also offers a range of "nutritional values."

The young black male needs to consume the glorious food that God will put on his plate. The church home is part of the main course for men. Salem Baptist Church, my church home, has helped me to develop an image of what kind of man I would like to become: a man who is loving, caring, and responsible and who, most importantly, possesses a deep love for his Lord and Savior Jesus Christ.

Many young black teens today are consuming too many of the unhealthy foods the world has to offer and neglecting the nutrition being served up in the church. I always listened to the popular music that was played on the radio until I really began to analyze the messages that some artists were giving, telling us young brothers to idolize the materialistic things in life. I was confused, so I looked to God for the answer.

Within the next two months I began to listen to more positive music. A lot of rap artists write about their love for money and riches, corrupting the minds of some young brothers to the extent that they even begin to worship an eighty-dollar T-shirt or three-hundred-dollar pair of pants. Yet there are other artists, many of whom are not receiving the constant radio airplay, who talk about their love for the culture and the movement of black people. Some of these hip-hop artists deliver to us young black males a good portion of nutritious dinner— groups such as Black Star, which gives us messages about respecting our sisters and calling for self-determination in the African American community. During this same time period, I also began to listen to a lot of Gospel music, which gives me another meal for the day with artists such as Donnie McClurkin, who tells us that we must stand and trust in God through all the troubles in our lives.

As young black Christian men, we need to possess the knowledge and be prepared to take care of our families. We have to respect and love our sisters. We need to deliver the message of the Lord and be a friend to all of our brothers. We must unite and lift up our brothers who are consuming too much junk food and fat, and deliver to them nutritious portions of meat.

, , ,

ON THIS DAY: *Thank God for all he has done in your life, especially for the people the Lord has brought into your life, who serve your daily bread, and for your church home, where you receive your good meat.*

Kenneth C. Hill

INTEGRITY BEFORE HONOR

The LORD said to Satan, "Have you considered my servant Job? There is no one like him on the earth, a blameless and upright man who fears God and turns away from evil. He still persists in his integrity, although you incited me against him, to destroy him for no reason." (Job 2:3)

In the story of Job, it appears that Satan is after Job's possessions, but that's not truly what he wants. He is after Job's integrity, his character, and his sense of self-worth. Today as Christian men we will find our integrity challenged as never before. Our society already has a concept of what young African American males are like. The picture has been painted that we will lie, cheat, steal, and compromise. The media shows deception and demise among us.

Can God still use us as testimonies? With all that we go though in our walks, will we hold fast to our integrity? With our families, will we be transparent? On our jobs, will we refuse to compromise our values? In our minds, will our thoughts remain pure? In monetary situations, will we be honest? Are we men of our word?

Job was tested and did not give up. In reward, God gave Job twice as much as he had before, but the most treasured possession he retained was his integrity.

, , ,

PRAYER: *Lord, help me to be a man full of integrity. Help me not to give in to compromise, in spite of what is before me, and help me to act purely and honestly in everything I do. Amen.*

John A. Morton

≋

GOD'S AMAZING GRACE

The child grew and became strong,...and the favor of God was upon him. (Luke 2:40)

In 1926 in a small town in Orange County, Virginia, a young mother struggled with a difficult pregnancy. She gave birth with the help of a midwife, but it was obvious that the baby was experiencing medical problems. There were no telephones in the home, so both the mother and child were taken by horse and wagon to the nearest hospital.

Upon their arrival, their worst fears became reality when the doctor said that nothing could be done to save the baby's life. The mother was devastated, but she never lost faith in God's amazing grace. She prayed all the way home. She was determined that, with the help of her husband and mother, she would save the life of her child. After a lot of prayer and some simple home remedies, the baby began to show gradual but steady improvement.

Today, that baby is alive and well. He graduated from college and worked for thirty years in the Philadelphia school district. He is currently retired and an active member of the Salem Baptist Church of Jenkintown, Pennsylvania. This is a true story of the amazing grace of God, who is able to do all things well. God and God alone holds the master plan for our lives, and he is truly a miracle worker.

I have learned through the years that I must wait patiently for God to work in my life, because it is God, not humankind, who makes the final diagnosis.

, , ,

ON THIS DAY: *I will remember to rely on the amazing grace of God, because his grace is all I need to sustain me in any situation I encounter.*

Jeremy Smith

FOR YOU ARE GREATLY BELOVED

At the beginning of your supplications a word went out, and I have come to declare it, for you are greatly beloved. So consider the word and understand the vision. (Daniel 9:23)

What was it about Daniel that prompted the archangel Gabriel to make such an honorable remark? By the time we get to the tenth chapter of the book of Daniel, Daniel has lived a long, productive, and faithful life for God. His people had long been held as captives of Babylon, where they had been forced not only to leave their homeland and become slaves, but also to worship the Babylonian gods and accept their captors' idolatrous culture. Daniel's career, however, was marked with godly resistance. He refused to eat food outlawed by God, and God blessed him. He refused to obey the law that required all the inhabitants of Babylon to pray to an idol, and God protected him in the midst of the lions' den. While under great pressure to succumb to Babylon, Daniel stayed faithful and worshiped God alone.

Because of his faithfulness to God in the midst of his people's subjugation, Daniel not only made a name for himself in Babylon, but, more importantly, he made a name for himself in heaven. Gabriel's words suggest that Daniel's name was well known by God and his heavenly host. When Daniel prayed, God immediately dispatched Gabriel. In fact, Daniel did not even have time to finish his prayer before Gabriel showed up to offer help! Clearly Daniel was beloved of God.

The man who is greatly beloved in heaven stands for God even in the midst of oppression. The man who is greatly beloved in heaven refuses to let anything disrupt the supernatural dialogue that takes place between man and his Maker during prayer. Let it be our goal to have a walk with God so close that we, like Daniel, are greatly beloved in heaven.

, , ,

PRAYER: *Lord, I pray that you would help me be committed to you in the midst of trials. Pull down* *every idol in my life that separates me from you, and give me the courage to be like Daniel, who did great things through your power and was called greatly beloved in your courts. Amen.*

Rayshad A. Holmes

THE WHOLE TRUTH

"If any want to become my followers, let them deny themselves and take up their cross and follow me."
(Matthew 16:24)

The saints lied!
They didn't tell the whole truth about this thing
    called a Christian life.
Nobody told me that in order to save my life, it
    would, in fact, cost me my life.
They failed to mention that a loving God would
    obligate me to love my enemies as well.
They forgot to inform me that living a life pleas-
    ing to God means routinely denying myself
    the things that my flesh regularly craves.
The saints lied!

But I am consoled in knowing that God never
    lies, never distorts the truth.
In the Word, God says that the hardships of the
    righteous will be many, but God will deliver
    us out of all of them.

So why wasn't this information printed in the welcome packet when I joined the church?
Why wasn't there a support group announcement for those of us who had issues with our new lives?

Allow me to set the record straight:
Living for God is a daily quest to do that which God has commanded in the Word.
It seems easy.
But your membership in the body of Christ obligates you to the war already in progress against the enemy.
Your talents, gifts, and abilities no longer belong simply to you, but are redesigned to aid in the upbuilding of God's kingdom.

There will be days when you are confused, comfortless, and confounded.
There will be weeks when you are forced to fast in hopes of being made better.
There will be seasons of valley experiences and occasional mountain encounters.
People will desert you as a result of the choices and decisions you make.

You will be labeled as a result of the moral code to which you now subscribe.

But rest assured, my friend, that you have made the best decision.
The recompense of the Christian life far outnumbers the sacrifice.

, , ,

PRAYER: *Father God, in the midst of hard times, I thank you. In the midst of my tears, I thank you. Even now, I recognize that serving you is not an easy task. Many are called, but few are chosen; thank you for choosing me. Now, God, I ask that you would endow me with the strength and determination to continue in this fight. Where it has been hard, I pray that you would make it easy. Give me the fortitude to keep on going when I would rather give up. Direct me and deliver me. I cannot do this without your help. In Jesus' name I pray, Amen.*

James L. Bumpus

KNOWING AND
DISCLOSING SELF

Jesus, knowing that the Father had given all things into his hands, and that he had come from God and was going to God, got up from the table, took off his outer robe, and tied a towel around himself. (John 13:3-4)

In recent years, the importance of and the effectiveness of servant-leadership has been emphasized in informal discussions, seminars, workshops, and various texts. The idea of servant-leadership dates back to the times of Jesus and is an important one for several reasons. Certainly among those reasons are its divine origin and adaptation in the New Testament church practice. Jesus used this model in teaching his disciples. The writer of the New Testament books Ephesians, Philippians, and Thessalonians refers to the principles that characterize the model of servant-leadership as well.

The effectiveness of servant-leadership as a principle for a community leadership model is

———

102

easily identified. This is most clearly seen in its corporate and empowering nature.

The community benefits of servant-leadership are many. However, this model demands much of the user, as is revealed by Jesus in the John 3:1-21 passage. Simply stated, one must know self. Self must be known and disclosed in the serving community.

For a leader to empower others, he must know several things about himself.

First, the leader must have more than a general awareness of who he is. As Na'Im Akbar states in his book, *The Community of Self,* "Knowing ourselves is a fundamental aspect of assuming personal power and effectiveness."

Second, the leader must know the responsibility laid on him.

Third, the leader must know from whence he has come.

Finally, the servant-leader must know where he is going.

These aspects of self-knowledge aid greatly in the necessary practice of self-disclosure in the serving community. The disclosed self is open. One's motives, desires, and objectives are clear. It means that the light of God's will shines through one's life as bright light shines through a transparency. As leaders in our communities, families, places of business, and worship centers, we must accept the responsibility of self-disclosure in servant leadership.

, , ,

PRAYER: *Today I will seek to overcome the fear of self-knowledge and be open to the many benefits of self-disclosure as a servant-leader. God, grant me to know my true self and give me the courage to deal with the revealing of who I am to others around me. Amen.*

James E. McJunkin Jr.

IN THE MEANTIME: A MEDITATION FOR AN ANXIOUS HEART

"To be able to give up the initiative over your own life; to yield at the core of one's self, the nerve center of one's consent to God; and to trust the act itself… is dealing with the most difficult thing in religious commitment." —Howard Thurman

Living in the meantime, the place that's in between the past and the future, would be exciting if only I would trust. While God lines up the particulars of my destination, I am often given meaningful tasks to accomplish. While our Lord reconfigures the realities of the universe, my hands need not be idle nor my heart be anxious. It is only at the nexus between stepping from the present into the future that I glimpse the unfolding purpose of the meantime.

I should rest easy, for surely the shepherd is preparing the table before me. It may be that in the meantime I am to develop the footing to stand on the steep hillsides of green pastures. What is more, I may be gathering the tools needed for work in the season that will soon unfold. Once again, I am invited to wait on the Lord in good courage.

꘏ ꘏ ꘏

PRAYER: *Lord, help me to stay focused on the present and not worry about the future, and help me to rest easy in the meantime. May I rejoice and experience the table before me, for it is abundantly sufficient, as you have promised. May I remember to trust you to lead me along paths that only you can prepare. Amen.*

Arlander Adamson Jr.

≋

WHO'S TEACHING, WHO'S BUILDING?

*"And you, Ezra, according to the God-given wisdom
you possess, appoint magistrates and judges who may
judge all the people in the province Beyond the River
who know the laws of your God; and you shall teach
those who do not know them."* (Ezra 7:25)

Our young men today are natural-born warriors, but being without God allows them to
work and war for the enemy, against themselves
and against the village. Our young men are
seeking to fight for justice, but they don't know
what justice is because being just requires
morality, and morality emerges from the village—the community of God—and without the
village there is no knowledge, and without
knowledge the people perish.

My brothers, knowledge comes from God,
and it is God who stands at the center of the village. In the village are found primary role models (e.g., siblings, relatives) from the primary

family structure, and it is out of the family structure that our moral training emerges: "Train children in the right way, and when old, they will not stray" (Proverbs 22:6). In that training, children should be raised up in the particular gift and its purpose; otherwise, they will be at risk for using that gift in service for the enemy.

Have our young men been trained up in the right way, or have they rebelled against the way? Whatever the case may be, we need some Ezras to rebuild the walls and reorganize the village to stand once again for justice and the law of God.

It's time! Our villages across the country have become a battleground in struggle against the enemy, and we stand in the church building and disregard the church outside the building where the second pulpit lies dormant. Our young brothers are out in the second pulpit and need some primary role models—some Ezras and maybe some Nehemiahs, too—who know God and who are willing to become that village.

If God has empowered you with the gift of teaching and building, I charge you to tend to the village that huddles beyond the church walls. Ezra, where are you? Israel's sons are in trouble!

, , ,

PRAYER: *"O LORD God of heaven,…Remember the word that you commanded your servant Moses, 'If you are unfaithful, I will scatter you among the peoples; but if you return to me and keep my commandments and do them, though your outcasts are under the farthest skies, I will gather them from there and bring them to the place at which I have chosen to establish my name.'" (Nehemiah 1:5,8-9)*

Gordon S. Houston

REDEEMING LOVE

"For God so loved the world that he gave his only Son, so that everyone who believes in him may not perish but may have eternal life." (John 3:16)

Brother to brother, you are my brother. We have the same Savior. We have the same God and the same Holy Spirit. We are members of the one body of Christ. In my lifetime, we have been called Colored and we have been called Negroes. Now we are called African Americans or black.

But I ask, just who are we? Does anybody really know? Or are we what others want us to be for their own conveniences and consciences? I have wondered about this for a number of years as others endeavored to tell me who they think I am. When I was young, my mother wanted me to have my hair always neat, to appear well-groomed in the presence of white people. I resented being defined in the terms of what the Caucasian people thought about my race. I resented my grandfather being called "uncle," or my grandmother "auntie," as others of the so-called superior race greeted them. Even today, my brother, you may find that some of your actions are determined by what you, or some-one in your family, thinks about the other race's expectations for you. For me this is a tragedy. It is a crying shame!

How have I come to grips with these devas-tating realities? Well, by the grace of a loving God and a merciful Savior, I have, in large meas-ure, overcome the race issue, although you and I both are faced with it almost every day of our lives. It is in our homes, on our televisions, in our newspapers, at our playgrounds, in our movie theaters, in our churches, and at our places of work.

What have I done to overcome this issue? First, I have believed on the Lord, Jesus Christ. Second, I have confessed him as my Lord. Third, somewhere along the journey of life I realized that God did not love only Caucasians. He loves me, too, and he loves you. To be loved is to be of value to someone, and you and I are of immeas-urable value to God.

, , ,

ON THIS DAY: *I boldly confess, without shame or apology, that God loves me and values me. With the love of God in me, poured out in my spirit, I am empowered to love others and to love myself. Thanks be unto God!*

E. Anthony Preston

≋

SEDUCTION REFUSED, SALVATION RECEIVED

"I came that they may have life, and have it abundantly." (John 10:10)

, , ,

"What no eye has seen, nor ear heard, nor the human heart conceived, what God has prepared for those who love him." (1 Corinthians 2:9)

Six-figure salaries, yachts, Caribbean condos, executive-level suites, Lear jets, high-tech computers, Rolex watches.... Get the picture? From a material perspective, life in America can be great. Yet while the things on this list, in and of themselves, are not evil, the apostle Paul makes it clear that life is so much more than the posession of mere physical wealth.

You see, although Paul spent time in Corinth, he refused to remain there. Corinth was where the up and coming wanted to be. Its influential residents enjoyed fine homes and gardens, resorts, libraries, coliseums, and art museums—

all the envy of the neighboring communities. Yet Corinth was a cosmopolitan steeped in sensuality, overflowing with enough vice and sin to rival any contemporary city of our time.

It was in this social climate that Paul announced he would take large living over living large any day. You already know what living large means, and large living can be understood through Jesus' declaration, "I came that they may have life, and have it abundantly" (John 10:10). In a nutshell, it's not what I have around me that counts, but Who it is who is in me. When our human wisdom tells us to stay in Corinth, God's wisdom counters with, "What no eye has seen, nor ear heard, nor the human heart conceived, what God has prepared for those who love him" (1 Corinthians 2:9). While I believe that this verse is written primarily with heaven in mind, we should also be reminded that God wants to serve us some "pie" here on earth as well.

Warriors, the apostle Paul's commitment to preach and live God's truth began and ended with faith. Faith coupled with the work of God's Spirit spells weighty results in kingdom-building. As African American men, we must quickly prioritize our values and communicate God's truth to our families and community so that we might live large as children of God.

, , ,

PRAYER: *Father, help me to desire and seek out your values for my life. In Jesus' name, Amen.*

Darryl D. Sims

≋

LONGSUFFERING

For in hope we were saved. Now hope that is seen is not hope. For who hopes for what is seen? But if we hope for what we do not see, we wait for it with patience. (Romans 8:24-25)

Waiting for something we want is one of the hardest things in life to do, yet we spend a good deal of our lives waiting. In some cases this waiting is only for a moment; in other cases it is for days, weeks, months, or even years. No matter how commonplace waiting might be, we still struggle with the reality of it. Waiting seems like inaction, as though we were surrendering to passivity, which is the exact opposite of how we as men are taught to behave.

In this passage, beginning at verse 22, Paul empathizes with how hard it is to wait, to endure hardships, trials, and disappointments before we can attain that which has been promised to us. And yet Paul urges us to have hope, to "groan inwardly while we wait" for the fulfillment of the promise of the complete redemption of our bodies (verse 23). Paul suggests that this waiting is not a passive exercise, but an active one in which we play a decisive role.

Paul compares our waiting to the pains of childbirth. Those of us who have witnessed our wives, sisters, mothers, or close friends go through pregnancy have observed the activity of waiting up close. During the pregnancy, the hoped-for child is developing inside the mother's body, but the mother does not simply sit and wait to give birth. During this time, she is preparing herself and her household for the arrival of the infant, the expected hope. The nursery is made ready; the crib is purchased and assembled; diapers, bibs, and bottles are stockpiled; birthing and exercise classes are taken to better prepare the body to deliver the child. And all this activity is undertaken with an attitude of patient expectation. The mother hopes for what she does not yet have but knows is coming, and she waits for it patiently and actively. Waiting becomes synonymous with expectant preparation.

Likewise, brothers, we must exhibit the same activity of waiting. We must prepare ourselves to give birth to that which has been planted within us. The delivery is coming, certainly, but it is the extent of our expectant preparation, of our active waiting, that will determine how we endure until the fulfillment of our hopes arrives.

, , ,

PRAYER: *Dear Lord, help me to realize how productive waiting is and to therefore engage in it with patience and expectation. I know, Lord, that you are faithful to deliver what you have promised and that no matter how difficult the preparation, how painful the labor, how slow the delivery, it all will come to pass. Amen.*

Jeremiah A. Wright Jr.

≈≈≈

THE SILENCE OF GOD

"...and after the earthquake a fire, but the Lord was not in the fire; and after the fire a sound of sheer silence." —1 Kings 19:12

In 1 Kings 19, Elijah saw God answer him by fire. In the sacred story of faith, God had answered Moses out of the thunder on Mt. Horeb. At the Sea of Reeds, God had answered the people's cries for help with the wind that opened up a highway for the people to walk through and escape Pharaoh's army.

God was known for answering God's people by the wind, by the fire, and by the roar of thunder (the earthquake). When Elijah prayed, therefore, he was looking for God to answer in one of those ways—in familiar ways!

So it is with the prayer life of today's Christians. We have grown accustomed to the ways in which our faith tradition teaches us that God answers prayer, and we look therefore for God to answer us in the familiar ways. When we don't hear from God in the ways that we expect, we feel God is silent.

Worse yet, we feel that God is not answering us when we cannot hear from God in the ways with which we are most familiar. This verse from 1 Kings, the nineteenth chapter, however, tells us that sometimes God answers us through "a sound of sheer silence!"

Many times it is in the silence that God is speaking most clearly. What we need to do is to stand still, tune out the outside world, and listen to and for the voice of God in the silence. It is in the silence that sometimes God speaks the loudest!

, , ,

PRAYER: *Grant me the grace and the patience to be still and to hear you in the silent days of my life. Help me to discern the depths of your love when you speak to me in those moments of silence. Help me to be still, to be quiet, to listen, to learn, and to feel the warm embrace of your unconditional love. In the name of Christ Jesus I pray, Amen!*

Oscar Crawford

WILL WORK FOR FOOD

"But he replied to one of them, 'Friend, I am doing you no wrong; did you not agree with me for the usual daily wage? Take what belongs to you and go; I choose to give to this last the same as I give to you. Am I not allowed to do what I choose with what belongs to me? Or are you envious because I am generous?'" (Matthew 20:13-15)

My friend Jack called recently. He had been searching the streets for brothers who carried signs saying, "Will work for food." Jack found one man early and offered him a deal: a day's work for two bags of groceries. The man agreed.

Jack took the man to work, and then, he was off in search of others. He found another, offered him the deal, and the second man agreed. A third man was found near a corporate complex. My friend offered him the same deal, he agreed, and Jack took them both to work.

Jack did this all day. The last brother was picked up near the end of the day.

At the end of the day, Jack felt good about the deals he had made and the work accomplished. He called the men together and gave each of them two very full bags of groceries.

Jack had no idea what was coming. The man who had arrived first became hostile.

"What is dis?" the man demanded. "I worked all day and they get the same. Sumpem wong wid dis pitcha."

Jack was shocked. What had he done wrong? He was helping.

He said, "Your signs said, 'Will work for food.' You have worked. You have food for your family. I kept my word."

Some threw their food down, cursed Jack, issued threats, and stomped off. But, others were thankful. They could feed their families. And now, they had even more food to take home! They had their own two bags, plus a share of what had been left behind.

Your greatest satisfaction must come from the privilege to love others and not from the privilege of praise for loving others well. How others respond to us is on them. How we love others is always on us.

Good works will not guarantee you will be liked. Love yourself enough not to allow others to bring you down and make your feel bad for doing the right thing.

When you have done the right thing with courage, conviction, and integrity, be encouraged. Be secure. Be at peace. Be thankful for the privilege of making a difference in the lives of brothers who are in need.

, , ,

PRAYER: *Father, use me to be a loving blessing to my brothers who need to be loved and blessed. Amen.*

Rudy Dowe

≈

HOLD ON: EVERYTHING IS GONNA BE ALL RIGHT

We know that all things work together for good for those who love God, who are called according to his purpose. (Romans 8:28)

, , ,

Not that I am referring to being in need; for I have learned to be content with whatever I have. (Philippians 4:11)

, , ,

My brothers and sisters, whenever you face trials of any kind, consider it nothing but joy, because you know that the testing of your faith produces endurance; and let endurance have its full effect, so that you may be mature and complete, lacking in nothing. (James 1:2-4)

In September of 1987 I was in the right place at the right time. For twelve years, I had positioned myself to become the first African American district sales manager in my company's history. I had started as a sales trainee in 1975 and worked up to the position of administrative assistant to the regional sales manager. In August my company announced an early retirement package, and many district sales managers chose to take the package. One September day, the telephone rang and I was instructed to report to Fort Wayne, Indiana, as the new district sales manager.

A wonderful feeling of accomplishment had overcome me even before Rev. Dr. Otis Moss Jr. announced our relocation to our family at the Olivet Baptist Church. When he eloquently spoke about my historic accomplishment, referring to the days when men of color could only aspire to become conductors on the railroad, an immediate sense of responsibility overwhelmed me. I was standing on the shoulders of men and women who had preceded me to make my moment possible. I realized that I must build on their foundation for those following me.

Exciting days were ahead—finding a home for my family, meeting new customers, learning a new environment, and supervising my own office. My wife, Joslyn, immediately found a teaching position with the Fort Wayne school district. My children, Tracy and Ashleigh, made an excellent transition to their new school. We were living in an exclusive suburb with a private golf course, swimming pools, playground areas, and walking trails. We continued to praise God as we found and became active in our new church. While problems occasionally confronted us, life was so good that I sometimes pinched myself to make sure that I was not dreaming.

Then suddenly, on April Fool's Day 1990, it was over! The regional sales manager personally delivered to me the shocking news that the Fort Wayne district sales office was closing. He instructed me to report to Detroit, Michigan, as an assistant district sales manager. In Detroit, I soon discovered the difficulties of being supervised by someone with less experience and training than I had. Resignation was not an option because I firmly believed that God had placed me with this company.

For fifteen months, I struggled with my dilemma, with the same questions and answers bombarding me daily: Why was I demoted? I had more experience and training than others. What did I do wrong? I couldn't point to any outstanding mistakes. Who was out to get me? I didn't

offend anyone. How did it happen? I had estab-
lished a good network to prevent it. Where were
my mentors to protect me? Upper management
knew about my good work. Why was my office
chosen to close? My sales numbers were better
than many remaining sales offices. The questions
only produced answers that fed my bitterness,
turning me into a very miserable person.

Then, as I was jogging on one beautiful,
peaceful morning in June of 1991, I felt God's
presence assuring me that he would deal with
my issues and that he was preparing me for spiritual growth. At once, my burdens were lifted
from me, and I began changing my attitude by
meditating on Romans 8:28, Philippians 4:11,
and James 1:2-4. Immediate results became
apparent as I learned to accept my circumstances, with no desire to search for an explana-
tion. Although my physical situation remained,
my changed attitude restored the vibrancy in my
life, filling me with wonderful possibilities
because I knew God was in charge.

The demotion was necessary for God to
return us to Cleveland where we enjoy his many
blessings, of which I'll mention a few: reuniting

with the Olivet church family; Ashleigh tying the school record for the 100 meter dash; Tracy's team winning the high school state championship soccer game—he scored the winning goal; Joslyn being recognized for her outstanding teaching skills; and me becoming a deacon at my church, serving with an extraordinary pastor, preacher, and visionary, Rev. Dr. Otis Moss Jr. When adversity comes these days, I just say, "Hold on: everything is gonna be all right."

. . .

ON THIS DAY: *I will remember that my heavenly Father is always encouraging my spiritual growth. Sometimes it requires me to deal with adversity. Let me thank him for the challenge, for when it is over, I'll be a better man for God.*

Kirk Byron Jones

≋

ATTEND TO WHAT IS ALIVE INSIDE OF YOU

Then within me there is something like a burning fire shut up in my bones; I am weary with holding it in, and I cannot. (Jeremiah 20:9)

The late singer, pianist, songwriter, and arranger Donny Hathaway is one of my favorite artists. Hathaway was reared in the black church, and his music resonates with pathos and passion, suffering and hope. His voice is equally and intensely loyal to both the blues and the "blues breakthrough" reality of everyday life. Simply put, Donny Hathaway can make you cry, and he can make you shout for joy.

At the age of three, Hathaway began singing on stage with his grandmother, noted gospel singer Martha Cromwell. Back then he was known as Little Donny Pitts, the nation's youngest gospel singer. The youngster was a sensation, but the best was yet to come. The child prodigy felt something wonderfully amazing welling up inside of him, and at age six, Hathaway began telling his grandmother, "You should hear the music I'm hearing in my head."

What would have happened if Hathaway had been unable to hear the music? What if he had heard the music and not noticed it, ignored it, or paid little attention to it? In order for countless others to be blessed by the artistry of Donny Hathaway, he had to first honor and trust what was coming to life inside of him.

The great teacher and spiritual advisor Howard Thurman once advised a college graduate wrestling with several vocational choices, "Do what is on fire inside of you. More than anything else, the world needs persons who are on fire."

What's most alive inside of you these days? How can you pay more attention to it? Can you allow more time in your busy schedule to hear what is calling you? Maybe it is a new calling, or perhaps it is one too long suppressed and denied that, thankfully, continues to tease and taunt you.

Attend to what is alive inside of you. You are waiting; your call is waiting. In the words of one of Donny Hathaway's most magnificent musical gifts to us all, *To Be Young, Gifted, and Black*, "There's a whole world waiting for you."

, , ,

ON THIS DAY: *I will own my passions and my dreams. I will fan the sacred flame burning inside of me to do what God is calling me to do in sacrifice and in delight.*

Ivan E. George

THE COMEBACK KID

Get (John) Mark and bring him with you, for he is useful in my ministry. (2 Timothy 4:11)

My nomination for the "Comeback Kid" of the early New Testament church is John Mark. His life reminds us that setbacks are only temporary when our ultimate trust is in Jesus Christ, that being down does not mean being out, and that God always has another person or another way to enable us to accomplish divine will.

Acts 12 suggests that John Mark had been in the church all of his life. A local congregation met in his home, and his mother was a leader in that church. He was there when Peter was miraculously delivered from prison, and he must have been present during various times when Christian leaders shared personal stories about the life of Christ and recounted the new advances of the young church.

As a youth in the congregation, John Mark must have made a favorable impression. He was chosen to be Paul and Barnabas's assistant on their missionary journeys. But when the going became tough, John Mark abandoned Paul and Barnabas and returned home (Acts 13:13). He had signed up for the miracles and the glory, but he wanted no part of the struggles and the persecution. It would be a decision he would come to regret.

On the next missionary venture, Paul refused to allow John Mark to travel with him. Barnabas disagreed, and the argument over John Mark became so strong that Paul and Barnabas separated and went their own ways. Barnabas gave John Mark, his cousin, a second chance (Acts 15:36-39).

John Mark learned from his first mistake and took advantage of the new opportunity. Everything else we read about him is positive. Paul, who had rejected John Mark in Acts 15, would commend him in Colossians 4 and refer to him as someone who can be of great help (2 Timothy 4:11). In the book of Philemon, Paul lists John Mark as a fellow worker in the Gospel.

Perhaps the greatest sign of John Mark's comeback is the testimony he gives about the life of Jesus Christ. He had met many persons who had first-hand experiences of the Lord. He had seen contemporary Christians both withstand the storms of opposition and convincingly proclaim the lordship of Christ. So, he wrote his biography of our Lord—and today we know his story as The Gospel According to Saint Mark!

The life of John Mark has much to say about our Christian journey and the redemptive nature of God. Jesus Christ specializes in comeback situations. He turned sin into repentance, sickness into wholeness, death into life, and damnation into sanctification. Jesus is the secret behind John Mark's magnificent turn-around.

I nominate John Mark because he is symbolic of the many comebacks that I have experienced in my own Christian walk. Again and again, Christ has taken my shortcomings, my bad choices, and my failures and turned them into demonstrations of his grace and mercy. I nominate John Mark because he can be an inspiration for you, brother. When you conclude that hopeless, remember John Mark and the miracles Christ worked in his life.

, , ,

PRAYER: *Heavenly Father, you are in the business of turning frustration into clarity, pain into joy. You are the source of all the comebacks in my life. I long for my eyes to stay focused on you—on your plans and priorities—so that you can bring me back on this day and all days. Amen.*

John E. Jackson Sr.

A FUTURE ON DRY GROUND

Then the LORD said to Moses, "Why do you cry out to me? Tell the Israelites to go forward. But you lift up your staff, and stretch out your hand over the sea and divide it, that the Israelites may go into the sea on dry ground." (Exodus 14:15-16)

In the church in which I grew up we had this saying: "Take what you got and make do until your change come." As African American men, we have made significant advances in every field imaginable, except having faith in ourselves to educate our own children. We have entrusted the education and development of our precious future to people who don't know our history and don't know the God who met us by the river at night away from the master's sight. The stormy sea of material success without spiritual grounding threatens us in front, while the iron wheels of self-indulgence turn just behind us. We need to stop crying to God about what we don't have and use what we do have more purposefully.

136

Black man, you can still pray with and for your children. Let them see you acknowledge the God of history, the Ancient of Days. Black man, you can take your children to school and sit in class periodically. Let them see that you believe what you pray. Black man, you can still discuss what you will contribute to the liberation of our people instead of dwelling on how bad things are for us. Black man, whether they are your biological children or you are going through "Baby Mama Drama," you can still be an example to our young people of God's strong hand. Look at your hands and use them to help build a future of dry ground for our sons and daughters to walk on.

, , ,

PRAYER: *Lord, enable us today to be an example of faith and deliverance to our children. Convict us that there can be no failure in this endeavor. Lord, there is too much at stake, and we need your power. Amen.*

Gerald K. Mayfield

≋

A FATHER'S FORMULA

*Train children in the right way, and when old, they will
not stray. (Proverbs 22:6)*

Nearly four years ago, my wife and I were
blessed with twins, a boy and a girl. It was a joy-
ous occasion, one of the greatest moments of my
life. God actually thought we were worthy of
being parents! Those first days watching our
beautiful children were so truly amazing that I
still well up when I think about them.

Soon, however, it hit me like a ton of bricks
that I was a father. I can't quite articulate what I
felt at that moment. You see, I had always been
Pat and James's son, not someone's father. I
began to realize all of things large and small that
I had taken for granted as a child. There were
countless things that my parents had provided:
guidance, when I thought I didn't need it; food,
when I thought I was hungry; shelter, when I
thought my room wasn't large enough; clothes,
when I thought I dressed like a nerd; and, of

course, love, when I thought no one cared. I realized that I had truly been blessed.

I realized that I now had the task of guiding my own children through life's hills and valleys. God had bestowed upon us one of his greatest gifts, and I was now responsible for developing the character of not one but two of God's creatures. *As a father*, I thought, *I must be aware of everything I do and say! I am now responsible for the physical, mental, and spiritual development of my children.* I knew that the responsibility of being a father should be undertaken with great deliberation, for every word said to a child counts. The thought frightened me. I asked myself, "Will I be a good father? Will my children love me? What do I know about being a father, anyway?"

I began to reflect upon what kind of father my dad had been to me, and I thought about the other men who had influenced my life. Most importantly, I remembered that the answers to all of life's questions are contained in the Bible, the source of fatherly wisdom. If you have a wayward child, look to Eli (1 Samuel 3). If you need a lesson in faith, look to Abraham (Genesis 22). If you need a lesson in a father's humility, study Joseph's relationship with Jesus. If you need help loving your children when they are doing all the wrong things, look to God's continued love to us as sinners.

Prayer also helps me to be a better father and to find the answers to the difficult questions that I face. Every day I pray to God that I might be a better father than I was the day before. The following prayer helps me through each day, and I hope it is a comfort to you also.

, , ,

PRAYER: *Dear heavenly Father, with bowed head and humbled heart, I come to you asking that you help me to be a good father, a devoted father, a Christian father. Lord, I pray that you grant me the wisdom to follow your instruction and to train my children up in your Word. Help me to bring my children to know Christ as their personal savior, and, Father, as I walk through this life, allow me to remember and model the behavior of my own father and the fathers in the Bible.*

Grant me the patience and understanding of the prodigal son's father; the faith, courage, and dedication of Abraham; and the humility of Joseph. Help me to be a friend to my children as my father has been to me, and help me to love my children as you love me.

Major McGuire III

≈≈

BIG BOYS DO CRY

They said to one another, "Alas, we are paying the penalty for what we did to our brother; we saw his anguish when he pleaded with us, but we would not listen. That is why this anguish has come upon us." Then Reuben answered them, "Did I not tell you not to wrong the boy? But you would not listen. So now there comes a reckoning for his blood." They did not know that Joseph understood them, since he spoke with them through an interpreter. He turned away from them and wept; then he returned and spoke to them. And he picked out Simeon and had him bound before their eyes. (Genesis 42:21-24)

On this day, I am eternally grateful to God for the freedom and liberty to express my feelings openly and candidly through tears, for it has not always been so. Let me begin by sharing with you an experience I had at the age of sixteen: the death of my father.

My father was 61 years old when I was conceived, and he took very seriously the call to fatherhood. He was a loving man, full of life, joy, and hope, and he could make people laugh at any time and about anything. He was respected by his family and seen as one who could and would give wise counsel to those who sought it. He was the patriarch of our family.

Like any young boy, I thought my father would be around forever. Illness slowed him down, however, and when he was 77 years old, death, that ultimate finality, interrupted his life on earth. I remember watching my mother weep without shame, and I remember how I sought to console her. As I sat in the front row of the church with my mother, I felt that I had to be strong for her, for myself, and for everyone around me. I couldn't express my true feelings openly, but why?

In a real sense, I had surrendered myself to the cultural and societal expectation for boys and men to be strong. I remember my aunt saying to me, "Junior, you have to be strong; you're the man of the house now." I embraced this expectation and made it my goal. No one suggested that I allow my feelings to flow. No one suggested that I talk about my father's death.

So many men are wounded within and do not know how to express their woundedness. Many carry the weight of a childhood nightmare still unresolved. Many have a low and unhealthy image of themselves. Yet many men still believe that "big boys don't cry." They have learned to "be a man" and hide their feelings. But they're wrong; big boys do cry.

Take, for example, the biblical character Joseph. We remember Joseph as the younger brother who was sold into slavery by his brothers at the tender age of seventeen. In Genesis 42:6-24, Joseph is now a highly respected official in Egypt, and his brothers have come seeking help during a time of famine. They meet with Joseph, but they do not recognize him. Joseph tests his brothers, and they squabble amongst themselves. Reuben, the eldest, believes they are being punished by God for what they had done to their brother, Joseph.

Upon hearing their discussion, Joseph, unable to control his emotions, turns away from them and begins to weep. He weeps over what happened between them so many years ago and over his brothers' acknowledgment of their sin.

He weeps out of love for his family. Joseph's tears reflect not just his humanity, but also his heart attitude. Here was a man who had more power, prestige, and authority than any man in the world at that time. And yet he never lost his ability to be tender, to show compassion, and to feel deeply for his family. One could say that Joseph was definitely a man's man, for he was powerful and successful, yet he was also a gentle man. He demonstrated for us that big boys do cry.

There are even modern men who have given in to the freedom of expressing their emotions. A few years ago, the New York Yankees, after winning the World Series, broke out in gleeful tears of celebration. And who can forget when Chicago Bulls star Michael Jordan bowed down on the court, hugged the ball, and wept?

Men, we are strong. We don't give up easily, and we hang in there when things are not going well. I believe, however, that it is when things fall apart that we, like Joseph, must allow God to lead us. We may have to weep while pressing on, but we ought to thank God for every tear that falls, because weeping can have positive results when God is in control. It is a God-created means for emotional release designed to prevent emotions from building up and festering years after the original pain. It is a characteristic of strength, as demonstrated by Joseph, and the water that proceeds from our tear ducts washes away the negative images that have flooded our lives.

We ought not forget that when Jesus arrived in Bethany following the death of Lazarus, a very dear friend, he wept. The supreme Son of God modeled for all of us that big boys do cry. Let us then learn to express our feelings honestly and candidly to the glory of God.

, , ,

PRAYER: *Our loving Heavenly Father, break the barriers that stand between us and our vulnerability. Teach us to cry again. Amen.*

Jeremy Smith

≈≈≈

FIGHTING INJUSTICE

Justice, and only justice, you shall pursue, so that you may live and occupy the land that the LORD your God is giving you. (Deuteronomy 16:20)

The book of Deuteronomy is addressed to the new generation of Israelites, who were destined to possess the Promised Land after forty years of wandering in the wilderness. The book is written primarily to laypersons, and in this particular section God lays out his expectations in regard to how the Israelites ought to pursue justice.

Justice is an intrinsic part of God's character, and God demands it of his people. Being just in the biblical sense means both being righteous and exercising fair judgment. This not only means actively helping the oppressed but also actively opposing those who cause oppression. We can be just because God is just and we are created in his image. Fighting injustice is not something we do in addition to our faith; it is a natural product of our faith in God.

We are able to overcome injustice because God is faithful and hears the cries of his people. As in the New Testament parable of the widow and the wicked judge (Luke 18:1-7), God will surely bring justice to his elect. As we continue to walk closer with God, he will make us more sensitive to the injustice that hurts his heart, and he will empower us by his Spirit to do more to confront those injustices for his glory.

, , ,

PRAYER: *Lord, thank you for the heart that loves justice that you have placed inside of me. I pray that you will help me to be more sensitive to the injustice that surrounds me, and I pray that you will empower me to help the oppressed and to oppose, by the power of your Holy Spirit, those who do injustice. Amen.*

Victor Parrott

≋

I SHALL NOT DIE

I shall not die, but I shall live, and recount the deeds of the LORD. (Psalm 118:17)

Until a few years ago, the seventeenth verse of Psalm 118 did not mean much to me. As far as I was concerned, it was just one more line in the poetry that makes up the Psalms. Then God spoke to me in that "still small voice," using the subtlety that is so much a part of God's character, and the verse took on greater meaning for me.

Before I heard the verse anew, I was mired in a victim's mentality. Being raised in a single-parent household by a mother who received only an elementary school education had lessened my self-esteem and confidence. Substandard housing and poverty had planted a seed of hopelessness that society watered on a regular basis. Consequently, it was easy for me to feel as though I had been wronged or short-changed.

When Psalm 118:17 came alive for me, though, my mindset changed. No more victim, but victor! That Scripture inspired me to look at my life from a new perspective, one that marvels at the transformation of a bastard child born in a ghetto with the odds stacked against him. Statistically, I was destined for a life of crime, drugs, alcohol, promiscuity, and unemployment, and I had unfortunately done my part in living down to those expectations. However, because of the compassion of a loving and merciful God, that so-called illegitimate child is now a college-educated certified public accountant, who works as an accounting manager at a major corporation, and is an ordained deacon and the head of a Christian family.

When I consider where I started and where I am now, I know that God has been good to me. "I shall not die, but I shall live, and recount the deeds of the LORD!"

, , ,

PRAYER: *Almighty God, you are my sustainer and my provider. I yield to your will, because I believe that you always want the best for me, even when I'm not trying to be the best for you. No matter what happens, I confess that you are God. I stand now in the gap for my African American brothers who feel* *the despair and hopelessness that I once felt. I ask that you would free them from the bondage of a mindset that causes them to feel victimized rather than victorious. This is my prayer in the blessed name of Jesus who is the Christ, son of the living God. Amen.*

Andrew L. Ford

DIVINE GUIDANCE

Trust in the LORD with all your heart, and do not rely on your own insight. In all your ways acknowledge him, and he will make straight your paths. Do not be wise in your own eyes; fear the LORD, and turn away from evil. (Proverbs 3:5-7)

My experience has taught me that when we learn to trust God fully and seek his guidance in all we do, we will discover a new outlook on life. We will feel a new security in our daily living, and we will be able to attain heights in life that at one time seemed impossible. God is a good God, a great God. He can do anything but fail. He has moved so many mountains out of my way. Oh, he is a wonderful God!

My God led and protected me through World War II in the States and the European Theatre of Operation. We were segregated, but he provided for me. He took care of my family and returned me safely home at the end of the war. My wife and I moved to Boston from

Roanoke, Virginia, in the year 1947. My God provided a home, employment, an educational opportunity, and a wonderful church. Oh, he is a good God!

During my many years of travel on this Christian journey, I have learned that there is no other way to a successful life than to be led by our Lord and Savior, Jesus Christ. With Christ, success is guaranteed. Victory over complex situations is assured. A fruitful vocation and a successful marriage are guaranteed. Your needs will be provided, and peace, happiness, and joy will be yours. And, best of all, a home in glory is guaranteed.

, , ,

PRAYER: *Lead me, guide me along the way.*
Lord, if you lead me, I cannot stray.
Lord, let me walk each day with Thee.
Lead me, Oh Lord, lead me.

Henry P. Davis III

≋

BROTHERS UNITED
FOR CHRIST

*To equip the saints for the work of ministry, for build-
ing up the body of Christ, until all of us come to the
unity of the faith and of the knowledge of the Son of
God, to maturity, to the measure of the full stature of
Christ. (Ephesians 4:12-13)*

It is beautiful to see African American men work
together in unity through Christ to build up the
earthly kingdom. This particular text in
Ephesians tells us that God has given to some
the gifts to be apostles, prophets, evangelists,
pastors, and teachers. According to Paul, some
are blessed with these gifts "to equip the saints
for the work of ministry" until we all come to the
oneness of faith and knowledge of Jesus Christ
as our Savior.

Throughout our history, racial unity has been
a powerful and often intoxicating call to action.
Yesterday, it was the fraternities and lodges that
gave a sense of belonging and made a person

feel larger than life. Many African Americans who lived through the civil rights movement can recall the pull to drop everything, get out, and do something. Today some "Gen X'ers" are drawn to the street gangs and the gangsta rap lifestyle for that same feeling of belonging and identification with a group.

The call for race-based action may not be the rallying cry that it was in the sixties, but the call to grace still rings stronger than ever. Jesus united twelve strangers and changed the course of human history, and Jesus still unites today. Every day we need to pray and work to strengthen our unity in Christ. Never take community for granted, and always be ready to encourage others. We have been gifted with the ability to call others to this magnificent brotherhood through Christ.

, , ,

PRAYER: *Lord, help me to encourage others to be united for Christ. I want to be one with you as you take full control of my life. Give me the strength to say no to the things that are evil and the power to stand on the strength of your Word. Amen.*

James E. McJunkin Jr.

DO YOU WANT
TO BE HEALED?

There was a festival of the Jews, and Jesus went up to Jerusalem. Now in Jerusalem by the Sheep Gate there is a pool, called in Hebrew Beth-zatha, which has five porticoes. In these lay many invalids—blind, lame, and paralyzed. One man was there who had been ill for thirty-eight years. When Jesus saw him lying there and knew that he had been there a long time, he said to him, "Do you want to be made well?" The sick man answered him, "Sir, I have no one to put me into the pool when the water is stirred up; and while I am making my way, someone else steps down ahead of me." Jesus said to him, "Stand up, take your mat and walk." At once the man was made well, and he took up his mat and began to walk.

Now that day was a sabbath. So the Jews said to the man who had been cured, "It is the sabbath; it is not lawful for you to carry your mat." But he answered them, "The man who made me well said to me, 'Take up your mat and walk.'" They asked him, "Who is the man who said to you, 'Take it up and walk'?" Now the

*man who had been healed did not know who it was,
for Jesus had disappeared in the crowd that was there.
Later Jesus found him in the temple and said to him,
"See, you have been made well! Do not sin any more,
so that nothing worse happens to you." The man went
away and told the Jews that it was Jesus who had made
him well. (John 5:1-15)*

Jesus walked past the pool and asked me if I
wanted to be healed. I knew him, and I knew of
his power. Of course, I said yes.

But Christ did not charge me to pick up my
bed and walk. His ability to strengthen my crip-
pled body was neither the question nor the
answer. The mat upon which I rested was not
external, but internal. I could not rise all at once,
and no outside force could heal me.

I would spend many more years by the pool
before I would locate the source of my discomfort. My journey was through the pain; there was
no way around it. Once isolated and compart-
mentalized, I saw bits of my reality. With denial
gone, I slowly began to face the truth, the very
facts of my life.

I'm standing up now, and someday I'll leap.

My witness is not of miraculous, instantaneous healing. Jesus did not heal me and walk away. In my story, Jesus sat by the pool with me. He troubled the waters within me, and as I stepped into the current, I found him waiting. We emerged together, and I became whole.

, , ,

PRAYER: *Yes, Jesus, I want to be made whole. Amen.*

Armat G. Woode

ON DEALING WITH
OUR OWN ISSUES

Now that you have purified your souls by your obedience to the truth so that you have genuine mutual love, love one another deeply from the heart. (1 Peter 1:22)

I really liked John. He had been a sheriff for some years, pursued a law degree, and now practiced law successfully. He was a charitable white guy, and we always spoke of the Lord freely when we were together. When we met for business, our conversation always turned to family, church, and missions, and this meeting started no differently.

As we spoke on this particular day, John shared his concern for the German exchange student who was spending her senior year with his family. "Kids are a little faster in Europe," he lamented, shaking his head. "I worry that she'll get into trouble during her stay with us. She had an older boyfriend back home, and I suspect she's somewhat experienced."

"What about the guys here? Anyone she's interested in?" I asked.

"Yeah, that's the problem. She doesn't think we know, but I'm pretty sure she and this one kid have gotten together, and I'm really bothered."

"Really! What kind of a kid is he?"

"He's actually a nice kid from a decent family—Catholic, I think."

"John, you just have to set some firm—"

"He's black," John interrupted. "That's part of the problem I'm having with all this."

For a moment I was stunned, but there it was. I immediately pictured a white, racist cop harassing innocent black folks, and our past Christian fellowship flew right out the window. I should have known. Why, he even looked like a—. I suddenly became aware of where I had gone and how quickly I had gotten there. What was the difference between John's attitude and my own? Quietly, the Spirit said, "Yes, that is how you are, too, and I came into your life to save you from yourself." John had at least acknowledged his struggle with race, even admitted it to me. "I would have taken a bullet for my black sheriff buddies," he said, "but this is something I was just raised to have a problem with."

"I'll pray for you," I said, not really knowing how sincere I sounded. "Pride is at the heart of it all, and I have my own issues," I managed. We finished lunch and I don't remember what else we talked about. We never got to our business.

A few days later, a radio message by Tony Evans titled "Strongholds of Discrimination" worked me over fairly well. I knew John needed to hear it, too. When my copies came, I called him to let him know what I was sending. He said he looked forward to getting it. It was good to hear his voice.

, , ,

PRAYER: *Father, save me from those attitudes that can so easily destroy me. In Jesus' name, Amen.*

Oscar Crawford

≈≈≈

LOVE DOES NOT ENVY

Better is the sight of the eyes than the wandering of desire; this also is vanity and a chasing after wind. (Ecclesiastes 6:9)

Dr. Keith A. Troy, pastor of the New Salem Church in Columbus, Ohio, preached a sermon entitled "Love Does Not Envy." His sermon made five points, the first of which brought to mind a memory. The point was "Stop comparing yourself to others." The memory was of an incident that had occurred some fifteen years ago.

I was serving as a chaplain in an Ohio state prison. Among the inmates was a Latino man— a muscular guy with great hair, a live smile, and a perfect complexion. It didn't take much to determine that sistahs would find this brother fine. And when I looked at myself in the mirror and considered his image in my mind, I was hatin' on this one. I was sure that if the ladies had to choose between this guy and me, I would not be the chosen one.

This envious comparison went on for days, perhaps weeks. The revelation came one evening as I was leaving work for the day.

When I heard the big door clang behind me, it dawned on me that it did not matter how good looking I thought I was not. My fine Latino brother had been convicted of a double homicide; he was locked up behind me, serving two consecutive life sentences for his crimes. But I— I was going home to my house to do whatever I wanted to do because I was a free man. I was free. And free is good. Free is very good.

At that point, being free was much more attractive and euphoric to me than my physical good looks—or lack thereof. I had to admit my self-esteem needed to be addressed. I was thinking too little of myself, of what I had to offer others, including the sistahs!

Comparing ourselves to others enslaves us to enemies that exist only in our minds. The struggle is all in our heads because we think we might be more if we were like someone else or if we had something someone else has.

Dr. Troy's sermon awoke that memory in me. May this devotion awake a comparable revelation in you. Be encouraged. Stop comparing yourself to others. You don't need to be like anybody but you!

, , ,

PRAYER: *Father, help me to appropriately love myself at all times, to honor myself appropriately at all times, and at all times to want to be nobody but the me you created. Amen.*

Dwight Davis

A LETTER TO MY SON

But strive first for the kingdom of God and his right-eousness, and all these things will be given to you as well. (Matthew 6:33)

Dear Son,

I was sitting in class thinking about you and our last visit together. I thought about the long, prosperous road ahead of you in life. I thought about what it means to be a developing, intelligent black boy growing up in the United States of America.

For me, it meant being robbed of my identity, having my "true" history taken away. It meant not knowing who my African ancestors were and being forced to identify with an image of a people portrayed as dumb savages. It meant searching for my identity but finding no roots, and it meant trying to plant roots into soil that rejected the seed. To be a developing, intelligent black boy for me meant I had to grow up without an adequate male role model in the home, yet I was still required to know what being a man is all about.

Although you don't have to deal with many of the difficulties that I wrestled with, being a developing, intelligent black boy still means you will have to deal with adversity from many sides. You might be labeled a bad student in class or told you have an inability to pay attention. Those same individuals will tell you that you are the best athlete in the school. This puzzles me, since a person needs intelligence to succeed at anything, including athletics.

You will encounter racism and jealousy. Much of it will come from older men and women of all cultures and ethnicities. They will dislike you because of your good looks, your intelligence, and your smile in the midst of trouble (your faith). Most of all, people will dislike you because you are a very confident young man who knows who he is and can accomplish anything to which he puts his mind.

Don't be angry about all this, son. Instead, seek to understand your brothers and sisters, and pray for them, for we know that prayer can change any situation. Remember, my son, to constantly seek God in all you do. The devil is always looking for intelligent and gifted black boys and men to destroy. Remember Matthew 6:33 and seek first God's kingdom.

Peace,

Dad

, , ,

PRAYER: *Lord, make me strong to stand against the trials of this life. Help me to remember to seek your kingdom above all else so that I can pass on your wisdom to new generations of developing, intelligent black men.*

Luther Holland

THE BURDENS AND BLESSINGS OF BOLDNESS

When they had brought them, they had them stand before the council. The high priest questioned them, saying, "We gave you strict orders not to teach in this name, yet here you have filled Jerusalem with your teaching and you are determined to bring this man's blood on us." But Peter and the apostles answered, "We must obey God rather than any human authority. The God of our ancestors raised up Jesus, whom you had killed by hanging him on a tree. God exalted him at his right hand as Leader and Savior that he might give repentance to Israel and forgiveness of sins. And we are witnesses to these things, and so is the Holy Spirit whom God has given to those who obey him." (Acts 5:27-32)

This story takes place right after the miraculous and powerful event known as Pentecost. Peter, John, and the apostles—bold, uneducated, ordinary men (Acts 4:13)—are now filled with the power of God and have been moved out by the

Holy Spirit as witnesses of the resurrection of Jesus Christ. They've received the charge to proclaim repentance and forgiveness of sin to all who believe in the name of Jesus. Through their actions, a man lame from birth is healed, and thousands believe in the Lord Jesus and are saved. Here is a scene unlike any other, filled with excitement and enthusiasm, wonder and amazement, exhortation and encouragement. It is the penultimate picture of revival, redemption, restoration, and renewal.

Yet this community of jubilee is laden with an air of tension and turmoil. Peter and the apostles have a face-to-face confrontation with the priests of the Sanhedrin Council, because the church authorities and members cannot agree on the church's vision. They can agree that something is wrong, but instead of seeking the Holy Spirit, they gather to replace God's servant, Peter. In this story we witness the miraculous power of God working through ordinary, uneducated men versus the exposed powerlessness of people who gained their authority by controlling their fellow believers. In this story we see an ugly picture of organized religion shuffling quickly to maintain its stature, even at the expense of the faithful and their servant leader.

Peter and John had to decide if they would obey the movement of God through the Holy Spirit or obey the wishes of faithless men who were on a power trip. The decision is obvious to a bold believer: We must obey God before human authority.

Scripture teaches us that as we do so, we will encounter both the burdens and the blessings that come along with our boldness. We saw how Peter and the apostles' bold decision to proclaim the truth brought opposition from the church leaders. Their mission of liberation disrupted the status quo, and the church leaders reacted negatively. The faithful were imprisoned, threatened, fired, and flogged for their boldness. You see, when you decide to follow Jesus, that is what you can expect from humanistic leadership. Following Jesus is liable to place you in direct conflict with humanistic folks who have no understanding of the power, presence, and potential of the Holy Spirit. With proclamation comes persecution; it is one of the burdens that responsible and accountable believers must bear if they are committed to serving God before serving a humanistic world.

When we obey God before human authority and church leadership, we must understand that our persecution may come from the most unlikely people. The final persecution of Jesus was an inside job, and so may be ours.

When we obey God before human authority, the powerful will seek to quiet the powerless. In Acts 5:28, powerful leaders gave Peter and the others a command to be silent, a charge previously articulated in chapter four. The religious elite were suddenly the apostles' greatest enemies, determined to silence them from preaching and teaching. We must be careful, because those we expect to support us may not truly be our friends.

However, when we obey God before human authority and humanistic church leaders, the power we have will ultimately prevail. God's Word will lead people to repentance and enable them to experience forgiveness of their sins (Acts 5:31). This is the blessing of boldness. There are many souls who will be saved, healed, rescued, and delivered by the power of God through our collective proclamation. Speak, Church, and rise up, people of God. Be bold, and the Lord will bless you mightily.

, , ,

PRAYER: *O Lord, it is a transforming moment when the righteous stand on and for your Word. Keep us ever in your care, O Lord, so that the burdens of boldness will bring about your blessing. Amen.*

Dumas A. Harshaw Jr.

THE SECRET TO STRENGTH

I can do all things through him who strengthens me.
(Philippians 4:13)

We grow up surrounded by images of strength
and power, and much of our early identity is
carved out by perceptions of how strong we are
as males. This begins in such innocent ways as
boyhood contests to see who can pick up the
heaviest weight, who can throw a ball the farthest, who can run the fastest, or who can take
the most blows to the physique.

It is not surprising, then, that most of us as
men measure our worth by physical standards of
strength. It is only by maturation that we learn of
the more significant elements of strength such as
good character traits, honest goals, and clear
intentions. When we submit our lives to Jesus
Christ in discipleship, we embrace another kind
of power that reflects the character of God.

In Philippians 4, the apostle Paul rejoices in
the gift of faith as he faces circumstances in

which his manhood is questioned. He says that he has learned the strength of being content no matter what he is facing in life, and he has learned to be content in the face of challenges to his physical strength. Through Christ, he has learned to be satisfied at all times. It is a true blessing to live in a state of rejoicing, no matter the fight or the fate. This knowledge of power gives to a man a sense of peace "which surpasses all understanding" (Philippians 4:7).

Strength in this context comes from thoughts of what is true, noble, right, pure, lovely, admirable, excellent, and praiseworthy. When these positive characteristics are put into practice, there is a newfound strength that really makes a man a man. This strength involves walking in such a way that God is pleased with our behavior because we treat the people in our lives with love and respect.

There is a secret to this kind of strength. It is not found in mind control, nor in muscle tone, nor in the accumulation of material goods, nor in the positions we hold and the salaries we make. Rather, it is found in the relationship we have with God through Jesus Christ our Lord. "I can do all things through him who strengthens me" (Philippians 4:13).

, , ,

ON THIS DAY: *I will recognize what true strength is and remember that the strength to be a real man comes from God.*

Rodney Ellis King

≋

"I Am Somebody!"

But those who wait for the LORD shall renew their strength, they shall mount up with wings like eagles, they shall run and not be weary, they shall walk and not faint. (Isaiah 40:31)

I feel that regardless of our academic achievement or economic status, African American males are still looked upon as inferior by society. If we do not conform to the dominant cultural norms, we are labeled as lazy, slow, and trifling. This labeling starts as early as preschool. When African American children do not conform to the Eurocentric educational system, they are said to have Attention Deficit Disorder or placed in special education, even though it's been proven that African American children learn differently than children of the dominant culture.

The African American male is a microsm of what's going on in our schools. Even now as we enter a new millennium, African American men still have to work harder than others to prove that they can perform on a level of success. Society is still doubting that an African American can be president or play quarterback in the NFL. Although some African American men have excelled in the corporate world, there is still a large number that haven't reached that status. If it were not for the Civil Rights Bill and affirmative action, many professional African American males, including Clarence Thomas, would not be where they are today.

I am reminded of a story about a farmer who raised an eagle on his chicken farm. The farmer raised the eagle as if it were a chicken, and eventually the eagle began to think it was a chicken. One day a stranger paid a visit to the farm and happened to notice that an eagle was acting like nothing but a chicken. The stranger said, "Let me take the eagle for a while, and I will show you that it is an eagle." The farmer agreed, so the stranger took the eagle and told it that it was an eagle and that it should stretch out its wings and fly. The eagle opened its wings and began to fly, but the farmer threw feed on the ground, and the eagle fell from the sky. The farmer said, "I told you the eagle was nothing but a chicken."

The stranger tried three times, and each time the farmer threw the feed, the eagle fell to the ground. Then the stranger took the eagle to a high mountain and told it that it was born an eagle and was born to be regal. He turned the eagle loose, and the eagle flew toward the sun.

As an African American male, I used to feel like the eagle that was taught to be something that it wasn't and made to feel inferior. Then, one day, I heard the voice of Jesus say, "You are somebody!" Now, because of my Christian belief, I know that I can do all things through Christ Jesus who strengthens me, regardless of what society tries to tell me. I am somebody! I am a child of the King.

, , ,

PRAYER: *Heavenly Lord, bring us the joy and confidence that comes from the realization, despite what society has said in the past and is still saying today, that "I am somebody!" Amen.*

Major McGuire III

RESPONDING TO
THE BLOWS OF LIFE

Those of steadfast mind you keep in peace—in peace because they trust in you. Trust in the LORD forever, for in the LORD GOD you have an everlasting rock. (Isaiah 26:3-4)

No one wants to experience the blows of life, situations and circumstances that wreak havoc and confusion in our lives. It is a fact, however, that we will all get caught in ill winds and turbulent storms at times. We should not despair, though, because those hard times make us stronger and more sensitive to the presence of God.

Even as I write, some folks out there are experiencing traumatic blows in their lives. There are also some who have led relatively trouble-free and calm lives, but I must be candid with those people. Life may be comfortable for you now, but experience has taught me that the blows of life are on their way. Not one of us is exempt from the trials of life.

When the hard times come, we may find ourselves asking, "Why did this awful thing happen to me?" The question "Why?" is not new to the human race, and certainly not unfamiliar to the African American male. Black men today are seen running vigorously with a football, jumping to retrieve a basketball, or standing in the batter's box, but we did not always know such success. Black men today are CEOs making six figures, but we did not always know such material prosperity. Slavery, Jim Crowism, unemployment, homelessness, mental illness, institutional racism, sexism, gang violence, substance abuse, and a litany of other ills have historically presented themselves to our people.

Besides the troubles we share as a race, there are other blows that come unexpectedly and unannounced. Some of us have lost a job, watched a marriage decay and end in divorce, been abandoned by a parent, faced rejection and loss. These blows threaten to discourage, denigrate, and depress us. They cause us to doubt our purpose for living, create havoc and confusion in our daily walk, and prevent us from achieving maximum strength and stability in the world.

How should we respond to the blows of life? I believe we have at least three options: First, we can drop our heads, droop our shoulders in despair, and give up. Second, we can blow up, lose control, and let our frustration come out in a fit of anger. What will these reactions achieve? Nothing positive, nothing redemptive, nothing encouraging.

So if giving up and blowing up are not the answer, what is? I believe that it is in "looking up" that we find the third option and our answer. We are not looking up to the stars and galaxies, but beyond them to our God. In Isaiah 26:3-4, Isaiah offers wonderful hope for Israel's future if God's people will just rely on him to help them weather life's storms. It is God who grants us perfect peace. This doesn't mean that the blows of life will cease. It doesn't mean that all of our strife, stress, and strain will come to a halt. There is, however, the promise of God's perfect peace in the midst of turmoil.

I myself experienced a significant blow when a neurosurgeon found a tumor resting on my optic nerve, causing blindness in my left eye. I was overwhelmed with concerns: Is this the end of the line for me? What about my wife and all of our plans? Will I regain my sight? Will I see our children grow up, graduate from college, begin their careers and families? Will I live to see our grandchildren? Then, by an act of God's grace and mercy, the prayers of others began to intercede on my behalf. I looked up to God and experienced a "peace that passeth all understanding" as I awaited surgery.

My brothers, the blows of life will come, but be assured that the same God who guided and stood guard over his people in the past is with us today. The Lord is eternal, sovereign, and immutable. No other support will fulfill our needs or sustain us when the blows of life rain down on us.

, , ,

ON THIS DAY: *I pause to thank God for the infallible Word, which is able to aid and help me through the blows of life.*

Kent L. Poindexter

MAKING SENSE OF YOUR WILDERNESS

Jesus, full of the Holy Spirit, returned from the Jordan and was led by the Spirit in the wilderness, where for forty days he was tempted by the devil. (Luke 4:1-2)

Have you ever had a spiritual wilderness experience, a time in your life when you just couldn't connect with your friends, your family, or God? The wilderness takes us to unexpected places, places of discomfort and loneliness with experiences that test our very beings.

Though daunting, these spiritual wilderness experiences are "training grounds," places where we have the opportunity to learn more about ourselves and about God. As you read Luke 4:1-13, put yourself in Jesus' place. Eventually the physical challenges become inconsequential; it is the spiritual challenges that prepare us for the journey ahead. These challenges provide us with survival skills, preparing us to stand for what we believe in, and to pray when lonely or tempted.

Our wilderness periods are also opportunities to confront ourselves. God puts the mirror before us and forces us to deal with what we see. No "frontin'," no putting the blame on someone else for our faults. If we are willing to see ourselves as we are, we can come out of the wilderness newly inspired, willing to let God be first in our lives.

In wilderness experiences, we are confronted with our beliefs when God allows us to be put to the test. Eventually, we are forced into a "close encounter" with God, an intimate relationship with the Holy One, the Creator.

And finally, through wilderness experiences, we learn God's will for us. God has made each of us with unique gifts, and in the wilderness, we can learn what God wants us to do with those divinely bestowed talents.

Take advantage of your times in the wilderness. Don't despair, but use them to grow as a person and as a child of God.

, , ,

PRAYER: *Loving God, help me to appreciate those times when you set me in the wilderness. Amen.*

Montague H. Pollard III

CAN THESE
DRY BONES LIVE?

Have mercy on me, O God, according to your steadfast love; according to your abundant mercy blot out my transgressions. Wash me thoroughly from my iniquity, and cleanse me from my sin. For I know my transgressions, and my sin is ever before me. Against you, you alone, have I sinned, and done what is evil in your sight,…You desire truth in the inward being, therefore teach me wisdom in my secret heart. Purge me with hyssop, and I shall be clean…Create in me a clean heart, O God, and put a new and right spirit within me. (Psalm 51:1-4,6,7,10)

I didn't know that I was dead, because I was still walking around. I didn't realize I was deprived, because I had gainful employment. Because I had friends, a good job, and solid ethics, I thought I was doing pretty well.

While I was in the military, my paycheck was often used for illicit nighttime activities. During my time in the service, I fathered a child and later married her mother out of loneliness. When challenges began to threaten my marriage, I resumed my immoral activity, and two more children later, I had a serious problem with alcohol and cocaine. I was still employed, but I was beginning to lose touch with reality.

After several tailspins and the loss of my family, I was brought to my knees by spiritual, as well as physical intervention. I began to read the New Testament my mother gave me the day I joined the military, and I was like a bone-dry sponge as I read it for the first time.

That was just the beginning. Ten years later I finally opened my heart wide enough for God to deliver me from what had become a very mean crack habit. I realized that I was suffering from a terminal case of spiritual ignorance.

Nowhere had I seen brokenness such as mine until I read Psalm 51, in which David expresses his most inner pain. As I studied the Word more and more, I learned that my painful past was due to my ignorance concerning the things of God. I remember begging God for wisdom, and, oh yes, he came through in a mighty way! I now have purpose in my life and a reason for living. I have received understanding through God's Word that provides me with a roadmap to this world.

I am now remarried in God's way. He is still restoring the years the locusts have eaten, but my head is held high by God's everlasting mercy. God's Word has shown me what love is, what it is to be a man, a husband, and a father. Now my dry bones are nurtured by the water of life, and I can really live.

, , ,

ON THIS DAY: *I will not think more highly of myself than I should, and I will work to strengthen my relationship with the Lord. I will move beyond the ways of the world, and I will continue to increase in kingdom principles.*

Jeremy Smith

I HAVE NOW COME OUT TO GIVE YOU WISDOM AND UNDERSTANDING

He came and said to me, "Daniel, I have now come out to give you wisdom and understanding." (Daniel 9:22)

Earlier in Daniel 9, Daniel was reading the Scriptures and noticed that God had revealed through the prophet Jeremiah that the desolation of Jerusalem—the time during which Daniel lived—was to end after seventy years. Daniel, noticing the calendar, immediately went to his knees, confessing his sins and the sins of his people, and entreating the Lord for deliverance out of the hand of the Babylonians. It is in answer to this prayer that Gabriel responds with the encouraging words, "I have now come out to give you wisdom and understanding." Gabriel tells Daniel of God's plan to free the Israelites from their bondage and to use Daniel to help carry out that plan.

When we survey Daniel's life, we see three factors that were present before this supernatural bestowing of wisdom and revelation occurred. First, God was ready to move. Second, Daniel spent time in the Word of God. And third, Daniel was devoted to prayer. If it had not been for those three factors, Daniel would not have been a part of what was to be God's remarkable deliverance of his people out of captivity.

These factors must be in our lives, as well, if God is to use us to deliver hope to the many who are oppressed around us. In regard to factor number one, God is always moving, so the question is really whether we are devoted to his Word and to prayer. Through study of God's Word and through prayer, God reveals his plans to and through us. When these things are aligned with God's movement, God can and will use us to do his work.

, , ,

PRAYER: *Lord, help me to diligently study your Word and meet you in prayer so that I may be pleasing to you and so you may use me to carry out your perfect plan here in this world. Amen.*

Raymond Jackson

≈≋≈

IT WAS GOD

O LORD, you are my God; I will exalt you, I will praise your name; for you have done wonderful things, plans formed of old, faithful and sure. (Isaiah 25:1)

In 1978 I went to a rehabilitation center to be treated for alcoholism. I had gotten to the point where I was drinking excessively every day, and I just couldn't seem to stop. In actuality, I didn't want to stop; I just wanted to "cut back." I thought I could learn to drink to "get mellow" and stay right there for the remainder of the day. That was my intention when I got to Livingrin; I was going to learn how to work the system.

Livingrin is a beautiful facility in Bucks County, Pennsylvania. There is a wooded area and a stream at the rear of the place. One afternoon, as I walked down to that area and sat on a bench, I began thinking about my life and all of the problems I had caused for myself and for others. Suddenly, I was on my knees with my head on the bench, crying uncontrollably.

When I stopped crying, I cleaned myself up and tried unsuccessfully to explain what had just happened. I began to realize that I no longer wanted to simply control the drinking; I wanted to stop it entirely. I have not had a drink since that day, and I know that God intervened, because he had something for me to do.

I had two teenage daughters from a previous marriage. God made it possible for me to get custody of them and allowed me to be both mother and father to them. I accepted Jesus Christ as my Lord and Savior, and we joined a local church. I truly believe that all along God was preparing me for my purpose in life. Today I'm an active member and co-leader of the men's fellowship in my church. I still have a lot of growing to do, but I also know that I can use my experiences to help younger men avoid some of the traps of the enemy and learn to trust in God to do wonderful things in their lives.

, , ,

ON THIS DAY: *I will thank God for all he's allowed me to go through, realizing that he was preparing me for the work I am to do.*

Rayshad A. Holmes

FOR THE MEN
WE HAVE YET TO BECOME

Do not be conformed to this world,
but be transformed by the renewing of your minds.
(Romans 12:2)

When I think of all that we can be,
All that we are,
And all that we once were,
I am amazed at the brilliance of God and baffled
   by our relentless pursuits in spite of what lit-
   tle life has given us.
From Kunta Kinte, to Langston, to Thurgood, to
   Spike, and Skip Gates,
We have taken little and continually made much.

But this quest has brought with it some chal-
   lenges, some setbacks, and some defeats.
Lest we forget Medgar and the other Mr. King,
   a.k.a. Rodney.
Our resilience, however, rests on the fact that
   God cannot lie.

In his Word, he promised that the last shall one day be first, and the first shall be last.

To each of you, I urge you not to become complacent.
Our struggle is unique, grueling, and far from over.
Somebody needs us.
We have lovers to protect.
We have sons and daughters to fight for.
We have grandchildren who will continue our posterity.

I urge you to continue to strive for that which is good.
Set new goals for yourself and work until you reach them.
Refuse to be refused.
It's just that simple.

, , ,

PRAYER: *Father God, I thank you for all that I am and all that you have willed for me to be. God, I recognize that there is more that I can do, and, with your help, I will do it. I thank you for blessing me because of, and loving me in spite of. Now, God, I ask that* *you would help me to take from life all that is mine. Teach me your ways that I might in all things represent the work of your hands. I ask that you endow all of my brothers with this quest. You didn't put us here simply to occupy space. Thank you for this and a whole lot more. In Jesus' name, Amen.*

E. Anthony Preston

THE PAYOFF OF A GOOD REPUTATION

Remember the word that you commanded your servant Moses, 'If you are unfaithful, I will scatter you among the peoples; but if you return to me and keep my commandments and do them, though your outcasts are under the farthest skies, I will gather them from there and bring them to the place at which I have chosen to establish my name.' They are your servants and your people, whom you redeemed by your great power and your strong hand. O Lord, let your ear be attentive to the prayer of your servant, and to the prayer of your servants who delight in revering your name. Give success to your servant today, and grant him mercy in the sight of this man! At the time, I was cupbearer to the king. (Nehemiah 1:1-11)

The value of a good name is precious beyond words. In fact, I contend that all our possessions are worth nothing if we have compromised our reputations and the testimonies of those on whose shoulders we have stood.

At the funeral of a deceased family member, I shared how bearing the Preston name had kept me out of jail on at least one occasion. When a white police officer pointed his gun at my head, I found relief when I told him who my kinfolks were. I don't know why the names of my relatives impressed him, but I was grateful for their effect. That night I came to realize as never before the importance of gaining (and keeping) a reputation for being respectful, honest, and courteous.

Nehemiah was the cupbearer to King Artaxerxes, and the two spent significant time together. The king's very life depended on being able to trust Nehemiah, and for years, Artaxerxes had been able to observe that Nehemiah was indeed a godly man. Through Nehemiah, the king saw that God gives direction and inner peace to those who are faithful. For this reason, when Nehemiah made a request, Artaxerxes assumed it was good and right, and he sanctioned it. Because of his good name and influence with the king, Nehemiah was able to change the course of Jewish history.

Every day, each of us will in some way influence those around us. By living godly lives and protecting our reputations, we enable ourselves to influence others in positive and life-changing ways. Nehemiah had no built-in advantage, but he did have love, obedience, and faithfulness. Be assured, brothers, that when we mirror these good qualities, the things we can accomplish will be unlimited.

, , ,

PRAYER: *Father, I thank you for placing good family and friends in my life. I pray that you will enable me to be a positive influence on others. In Jesus' name, Amen.*

Clarence Christian Williams

LET THE LOVE OF CHRIST CONSTRAIN YOU

So if anyone is in Christ, there is a new creation: every-
thing old has passed away; see, everything has become
new! (2 Corinthians 5:17)

I grew up and was raised in a small town in
South Jersey. When I enlisted in the U.S. Army
two days after high school graduation, I had
already backslidden from my religious upbring-
ing. I was literally running from family, friends,
ministry, and myself.

While in the Army, I did what almost every
other man of color was doing. I drank, smoked,
cursed, fornicated, lied, stole, and cheated. I par-
ticipated in everything short of murder. Not
knowing that God's grace and mercy were being
applied to my life, I tried on my own to make a
turn for the better. The pleasure of sin pulled me
back every time, so I stopped fighting with
myself, gave up, and gave in to sin. But out of my
own mouth I said, "I'll get right with God when

I'm thirty" (because at age eighteen, thirty seemed really old).

After six years in the Army, I was ready to be a civilian again, but I was still the same sinner in a different environment. It took a back injury, weight gain, rehab, painkillers, and depression for me to get right with God. On June 21, 1997, in the midnight hour, God healed my back when I humbled myself in prayer. When I turned thirty, the Holy Spirit reminded me of my own words. My mother called and invited me to a revival at my old home church in South Jersey. I left my apartment in Delaware and went to the revival every night for a week. On the last night, when the speaker had an altar call, I rededicated my life to Christ.

Through a Bible study group at my workplace, I was invited to and joined a new church. While God was answering my prayers and blessing me with revelation, understanding, and wisdom, I was learning to deal with temptation and the actions of my past. I now know through God's Word that I am forgiven and am a new creation (2 Corinthians 5:17), and for the past four years I have stood on the promises of God in his holy Scriptures. I invite every single man to read, rely, meditate, and stand on the Word of the Lord, for only Christ can make us whole.

, , ,

ON THIS DAY: *I pray for all men that they might build character and faith to remain whole in the Lord, our God.*

James E. Sturdivant

≋

WHAT'S MISSING?

"And remember, I am with you always, to the end of the age." (Matthew 28:20)

Basketball star and rapper Shaquille O'Neal produced a recording called, "My Biological Didn't Bother." The song speaks of the pain he experienced when his natural father, under pressure to provide for his family, abandoned Shaquille and his mother. Shaquille tells, in today's language, of the struggles he endured while being raised by a single mother.

When Shaquille's mother finally settled into a relationship with another man, that man took an interest in the oversized, undisciplined boy and helped turn his life around. After much conflict and confrontation, the story had a happy ending: Shaquille O'Neal has become one of the wealthiest sports celebrities to date.

Despite Shaquille's outward success, his song still speaks of an inner struggle because of his missing father. Isn't that where many of us are?

We may be successful in the board room, on the golf course, in church, on campus, or in our homes. But what about when no one is looking, in the solitude of our thoughts? We've found a measure of success, but we're missing our fathers. Some of our dads were missing because of death, divorce, emotional absence, all-consuming jobs, or addictions.

Jesus reminds us, though, that no matter who or what is missing in our lives, a relationship with him can make the difference. Don't deny the anger. Don't act like the pain isn't real. Face it and confront it, not on your own, but with the help of your heavenly Father.

, , ,

PRAYER: *Lord, I admit I've been angry and empty because I have missed my father. Please help me to rely on you to make me complete. Help me to remember that you are everything I need and that I can be strong and healed with your help. Amen.*

Walter S. Thomas

THE COMMAND TO ASK

"Ask, and it will be given you…" (Matthew 7:7)

It is extremely difficult for men to ask for help. There is something in our nature that makes us think we can do anything and we know everything. We will not read instructions; we just begin assembling. We will not ask directions; we drive by memory. There is nothing more comical than watching a brother who needs help declare, "I can do it myself."

Too many men have concluded that they will be thought of negatively if they are in need of assistance. We equate strength and independence with manhood. If a man needs help, we think, then he is not strong and he is definitely not competent. Our ability to succeed is fueled by our need for praise, which affirms us and makes us feel that we have worth. Because of this, many men do not ask for help; they are afraid they will be denied the praise that comes with accomplishment.

Jesus cancelled that kind of thinking. He declared to the hundreds who heard him at the base of the Mount of the Beatitudes that it is senseless to expect ourselves to be self-sufficient. In fact, he gives what might be called a command: "Ask." That is hard for so many, but so necessary. God did not intend for us to struggle through life in isolation. He wants to be a part of our lives, giving to us all that we need to accomplish the tasks that are laid before us. He wants us to know at the outset of every task that he is available to empower us to do fully, brilliantly, and completely whatever has been assigned to our hands. Don't spend the day struggling with what you cannot complete, fix, or accomplish. Whatever it is, ask for God's assistance, and remember, "Ask, and it will be given you."

, , ,

PRAYER: *Heavenly Father, help us to understand that ultimately pride underlies our need to be totally self-sufficient. We need you, and we need one another. Break our pride. Teach us that it is okay to ask both for directions and for direction. Amen.*

Dale G. Caldwell

THE COMPASSIONATE TENTH

The fruit of the Spirit is love, joy, peace, patience, kindness, generosity, faithfulness, gentleness, and self-control (Galatians 5:22-23).

As the son of a United Methodist minister father and an elementary school teacher mother, I grew up with an understanding of the importance of a good education and of service to others. My father, who knew Dr. Martin Luther King Jr. and was active in the civil rights movement as far back as the 1950s, made sure that I knew how important spirituality and community service is to my identity as an African American man. The moral and intellectual foundation that my parents gave me enabled me to graduate from two of the best schools in the country, become a successful businessman, and help the less fortunate in the African American community.

Unfortunately, I represent only a small percentage of successful black men my age, a generation of people who have benefited from the civil rights movement but who are unwilling to spend considerable time using their expertise and experience to improve the lives of other African Americans. W. E. B. Du Bois discussed the growing importance of a black bourgeoisie that he called the "Talented Tenth." Unfortunately, the African Americans who are members of this well-off ten percent have not, on the whole, made much of an effort to help other members of our community who are suffering. I believe many members of this elite group have been seduced by material things and have ignored their spirituality. Therefore, I think we in the African American community need to identify a "Compassionate Tenth." This group should represent the ten percent of the African American population who feel a spiritual calling to advance the civil rights movement by sharing their faith, time, and money to help African Americans who are struggling spiritually, mentally, and physically.

As an African American man, I am continually challenged to balance work, relationships, spirituality, and community service. I often fail. However, I try my best. I have found that the fruit of the Spirit described in Galatians 5:22-23 has provided me with the spiritual guidance necessary to help those individuals in our community who are less fortunate than I am. The fruit referred to in the Bible includes love, joy, peace, longsuffering, gentleness, goodness, faith, meekness, and temperance. If more of our African American men attempted to demonstrate this fruit, then the African American community as a whole would be much better off.

, , ,

ON THIS DAY: *I will try to demonstrate the fruit of the Spirit: love, joy, peace, longsuffering, gentleness, goodness, faith, meekness, and temperance.*

through Christ…. Rea
scared! None of this s

Then, gradually,
began to feel a calm c
sat down beside me w
nervous in the least.
and reassuring presen
and said, "You don't h
I am with you always
world" (Matthew 28:2

The lesson? Next ti
you, remember that C
more than the whol
brother, take heart; by
with Christ, you will g
courage to face life in

PRAYER: *Heavenly Fat*
with me, that there is not
present. Regardless of the
are there to comfort and
especially in times of fe
there by my side.

men aren't supposed to be
-talk worked.

lmost imperceptibly, I
me over me. A passenger
o didn't seem worried or
 fact, he had a calming
. He simply turned to me
ve to be afraid. I told you
even to the ends of the
).

he life tries to intimidate
d is with you, and he is
 world against you. So,
ultivating a relationship
n comfort, strength, and
hy situation.

, ,

er, I know you are always
here I can go to escape your
place or circumstances, you
to guide. May I remember,
r and stress, that you are

CONCLUDING THOUGHTS

On the two-hundredth anniversary of the African American Methodist Episcopal Church, Dr. James Washington, the late African American genius who taught church history at Union Theological Seminary in New York, said, "After every revolution, those who have fought the revolution tell their story to the succeeding generation so that their children and grandchildren would know why they fought the revolution."

Washington argued that in the French Revolution, the American Revolution, and even the Haitian Revolution, the survivors of the revolution told their stories to their children so they would know why their foreparents had struggled, what they had fought for, and what they had learned. In other words, they passed on the values of the revolution to their children and their grandchildren.

Dr. Washington then shocked those gathered for the celebration of the AME Church's bicentennial by saying, "It is only in the African American story that we have failed to teach our children the values of our revolution. We have failed to tell them the story of our revolution. We have not written down nor passed on what it was we fought for and why it is we fought!"

Nowhere is Washington's indictment more telling than in the story of the African American male Christian! Many of our children think that the African's struggle for freedom in America started with Martin Luther King Jr. We have not told the story of Rev. Gabriel Prosser, Rev. Denmark Vesey, Rev. Nat Turner, Rev. Harriet Tubman, or Bishop Henry McNeal Turner.

We have not told our children the story of Dr. Gordon Blaine Hancock, Dr. Samuel DeWitt Proctor, Drs. Adam Clayton Powell Sr. and Jr., Rev. Alexander Crummel, or Bishop Charles Harrison Mason. We have not talked about the Christian foundation upon which Marcus Garvey built or from which Edward Wilmot Blyden taught before emigrating to West Africa in the 1800s.

We have not taught our children the story of Lott Carey, Desalines, or Gullah Jack. Our children do not know, therefore, the centrality of the role African American Christian men played in the freedom struggle from the seventeenth century to the present. *From One Brother to Another* is what we hope will be "a first step" in correcting the mistake that Washington points out that we have made.

These devotional pieces have been written by African American Christians who are a part of that "great cloud of [male] witnesses" who make up the African American church in the twenty-first century. It is from the hearts, lips, and lives of those African American brothers who make up our rich story that the soil was plowed up and prepared for the roots of faith that are shown on these preceding pages.

All of these men come from a rich legacy of strong African American Christian faith. All of them have flowing through their veins the blood of those whom Paul Lawrence Dunbar called "the Black and unknown bards!" There is a wide variety of faith traditions represented in these pages. There is a wide range of experiences in many different professions represented in these pages. There are persons with earned Ph.D.s and there are persons with no degrees whatsoever who write in these pages.

All of them are men whose lives have been claimed by Christ. They have been touched by the hand of One who has led them "over a way that with tears has been watered." They have a rich legacy to pass on to the future generation. It is our hope that what is offered in these pages will be the first steps in making sure that we do pass on to our children the story of our struggle and the way over which we have come.

It is our hope that the African American men of the church of Jesus Christ will find their voices to make sure that our children know the way of the ancient paths and learn how to walk in that way.

Thus says the Lord: "Stand at the crossroads, and look, and ask for the ancient paths, where the good way lies; and walk in it, and find rest for your souls."
—*Jeremiah 6:16*

ABOUT THE CONTRIBUTORS

≈≈≈

Arlander Adamson Jr. is a deacon and minister in training. His church home is Trinity United Church of Christ in Chicago, Illinois. As of 2002, Deacon Adamson has been eight years free from addiction.

Ed Bowman is a licensed clinical social worker in Chicago, Illinois, and chair of the counseling ministry at Trinity United Church of Christ, also in Chicago.

Michael Brown is an associate judge in the Circuit Court of Cook County, Chicago, Illinois.

James L. Bumpus is pastor of Tremont Temple Baptist Church in Macon, Georgia.

Dale G. Caldwell is assistant commissioner for the department of community affairs in New Jersey.

Gilbert H. Caldwell is retired after having served for forty-five years as a United Methodist minister in Massachusetts, Connecticut, New York, Pennsylvania, Washington, D.C., and Colorado.

Oscar Crawford is pastor of New Eden Ministries in Chandler, Arizona.

Wayne E. Croft Sr. serves as pastor of The Church of the Redeemer Baptist, Philadelphia, Pennsylvania. He is currently a Ph.D. student at Drew University in Madison, New Jersey.

Dwight Davis is a third-year, dual-degree (M.Div./ M.A. in Christian education) senior at Princeton Theological Seminary in Princeton, New Jersey.

Henry P. Davis III is pastor of the First Baptist Church of Highland Park, Landover, Maryland.

Victor M. Davis is senior pastor at Trinity Baptist Church in Columbus, Ohio.

Rudy Dowe is a husband of twenty-nine years, the father of two children, and most importantly, one of God's children.

Andrew L. Ford is a member of People's Baptist Church in Boston, Massachusetts, where he served in the music department for more than fifty years and where he continues as an honorary deacon.

Ivan E. George is executive director of the Ministerial Leadership Commission of the American Baptist Churches USA.

Lawrence Hargrave is pastor of The Church on the Hill in Rochester, New York, and director of alumni, church, and community relations for Colgate Rochester Crozer Divinity School.

Dumas A. Harshaw Jr. is senior pastor at First Baptist Church in Raleigh, North Carolina, and an adjunct professor of theology and religion at Shaw University and Duke Divinity School.

Kenneth C. Hill operates in the prophetic and deliverance ministries. He is a teacher, evangelist, and associate minister at Eternal Hope of Glory in Chester Township, Pennsylvania.

Luther Holland is ordained by the United Church of Christ and is senior pastor of the Congregational Church of Park Manor in Orland Park, Illinois.

Ralph W. Holmes has been an ordained deacon for more than twenty-five years and is a retired marketing representative for the Exxon Corporation.

Rayshad A. Holmes is a writer and lecturer dedicated to the mission of helping others through using his gift of humor. He is a member of Greater Mt. Calvary Church in Washington, D.C.

Gordon S. Houston is founder and pastor of the Christian Church in Philadelphia, Pennsylvania.

John E. Jackson Sr. is associate pastor of men's ministries at Trinity United Church of Christ in Chicago, Illinois.

Raymond Jackson is a member of Eternal Hope of Glory Church in Chester Township, Pennsylvania, where he preaches for the prison ministry, sings in the choir, co-leads the men's fellowship, and serves on the finance committee.

Kirk Byron Jones has twenty years of pastoral experience. He is assistant professor of Christian ethics at Andover Newton Theological School and the author of *Rest in the Storm* (2000) and the forthcoming *Addicted to Hurry* (2003), both published by Judson Press.

William J. Key is an MMBB field representative for the American Baptist Churches USA, region of the South. He coedited the first volume of *From One Brother to Another*.

Rodney Ellis King is pastor of Philadelphia Baptist Church in Philadelphia, Pennsylvania.

Gerald K. Mayfield is an ordained deacon and attorney in Philadelphia, Pennsylvania.

Major McGuire III serves at University Park Baptist Church in Charlotte, North Carolina, as director of pastoral care.

James E. McJunkin Jr. is executive minister of the Philadelphia Baptist Association in Philadelphia, Pennsylvania.

Marvin A. McMickle is pastor of Antioch Baptist Church in Cleveland, Ohio, and the author of three Judson Press books, including *An Encyclopedia of African American Christian Heritage* (2002).

William Miner, is a retired social science analyst and lives with his wife in Bridgewater, New Jersey.

John A. Morton is a retired teacher in the Philadelphia School District in Pennsylvania.

LeDelvin J. Peavy works as a project analyst for a major insurance company in Cleveland, Ohio, and is a member of St. Timothy Missionary Baptist Church.

James C. Perkins is pastor of Greater Christ Baptist Church in Detroit, Michigan, and founder of the Benjamin E. Mays Male Academy. He is the author of the Judson Press book *Building Up Zion's Walls* (1999).

Kent L. Poindexter is an ordained minister in the United Church of Christ and a consultant.

E. Anthony Preston serves as chair of the deacon ministry at New Salem Baptist Church in Columbus, Ohio.

Mimsie Robinson is missions minister at Bethel Gospel Assembly in Harlem, New York City.

Guy S. Schley is minister of missions and outreach at the Mt. Olivet Baptist Church in Columbus, Ohio. He serves under the pastoral leadership of Rev. Dr. Charles E. Booth.

Darryl D. Sims is pastor at Shiloh Baptist Church in Massillon, Ohio. He is founder and president of Evangucation Ministries and is editor of *Sound the Trumpet! Messages to Empower African American Men* (Judson Press, 2003).

Campbell B. Singleton III is minister of mission support for the American Baptist Churches of Metropolitan New York.

Jeremy Smith is a master's student of world religions at Harvard University in Boston, Massachusetts.

James E. Sturdivant is founding pastor of Faith United Ministries in Washington, D.C.

Walter S. Thomas is pastor of the New Psalmist Baptist Church in Baltimore, Maryland. He is the author of two Judson Press books: *Spiritual Navigation for the 21st Century* (2000) and *Good Meat Makes Its Own Gravy* (2000).

Clarence Christian Williams is member of Eternal Hope of Glory, the largest and fastest-growing church in Chester Township, Pennsylvania.

Armat G. Woode is a sales representative and an amateur tennis player who attends Grace Brethren Church in Westerville, Ohio.

Jeremiah A. Wright Jr., the editor of this volume, is senior pastor of Trinity United Church of Christ in Chicago, Illinois. He is the author of multiple books, including the Judson Press titles *Good News!* (1995) and *What Makes You So Strong?* (1993).

Donald Young serves as deacon and member of the sanctuary choir at the Trinity United Church of Christ in Chicago, Illinois, where he has been an active member for more than twenty-three years.

Future editions of
From One Brother to Another

If you would like to be invited to contribute to possible future volumes of *From One Brother to Another,* please send your contact information to:

> From One Brother to Another
> Judson Press
> P.O. Box 851
> Valley Forge, PA 19482-0851

57 (208
69
71
82
101
106
120
123
135
140
147
149
152
154
160
166
188
190
192
199
201
203